RICH, RARE
& RED

RICH, RARE & RED

The International Wine & Food Society's
GUIDE TO PORT

Ben Howkins

THE INTERNATIONAL WINE & FOOD SOCIETY

 AND

HEINEMANN : LONDON

William Heinemann Ltd
10 Upper Grosvenor Street, London W1X 9PA

LONDON   MELBOURNE   TORONTO
JOHANNESBURG   AUCKLAND

First published 1982
© Ben Howkins 1982
SBN 434 34909 7

Filmset by Deltatype, Ellesmere Port
Printed in Great Britain by
Redwood Burn Limited, Trowbridge, Wiltshire

Contents

List of Plates

Acknowledgements

I WOULD LIKE to thank all my colleagues and friends in Croft for their support, guidance and patience during the preparation of this book. George Robertson and Robin Reid particularly have been marvellous founts of knowledge that I have been fortunate enough to draw on throughout the past ten years. John Burnett has also given me the benefit of his vast technical knowledge, for which I am most grateful. Such is the nature of the port trade that I received unstinting hospitality and much time from my friendly competitors. Among those whose help has enriched this book are Joaquim Manuel Cálem and Alfredo Hoelzer, of Cálem, Antonio Felipe and David Orr of Cockburn, David Delaforce of Delaforce, Jorge Ferreira of Ferreira, Fernando van Zeller of Noval, Manuel Poças Pintão of Poças Junior, José Antonio Rosas of Ramos Pinto, Manuel Silva Reis of Royal Oporto, Tim Sandeman and Ian Sinclair of Sandeman, Michael Symington of Silva & Cosens and Alastair Robertson of Taylor.

I am most grateful to my secretary Moira Smith who has always been cheerful and patient at the typewriter. My veritable tower of strength, however, has been Pamela Vandyke Price, who all along has given her valuable time to encourage me with literary prudence and sound advice.

I am also indebted to all those friends whose enthusiasm for drinking port is so infectious; to those I.D.V colleagues around the world who have so kindly channelled information to me; to Alexis Bespaloff, who has kept me attuned to the U.S. market over a number of years; to Michael Druitt, whose silver port neck labels adorn the front cover; and to John St John, W. Roger Smith, and Louise Bloomfield for picking up this book and running with it.

To Manuel Zarralugui, Don Lovell MW, Charles Eve MW, and Richard Alloway of I.D.V. I would like to record a sincere thank you for their support. To Hugo Dunn-Meynell, an equally sincere thank you for the International Wine & Food Society's support.

For Clarissa

Preface

Oh, Plump Head Waiter at the Cock,
To which I must resort.
How goes the time? 'Tis five o'clock.
Go fetch a pint of port.

Dr Johnson, 1778.

THROUGH THE CENTURIES, port has responded well to tradition and wit. A glass of port to many of our forbears indicated a satisfying yet never-growing degree of self-indulgence. Passing the port around the dinner table was an enjoyable, manly pursuit. Now, happily, port has definitely become non-sexist.

Port epitomizes the conversational wine. You cannot gulp it, you enjoy it, slowly, with friends. That must be correct in today's frenetic world. Port has been going long enough to leave the quaffing business to someone else.

Belonging to the port trade is like joining a club. You abide by the rules and enjoy the competitive friendship. I so enjoyed the club that I wanted to give the port devotee an insight into the inner workings of the world of port. There is so much tradition willing to be harnessed; so much knowledge waiting to be sown; so dry a thirst that needs to be quenched, that this book is written expressly for all those who enjoy a glass of port whether at a formal dinner, watching television at home, at a bar or as an aperitif.

I have tried to capture the excitement of port as we see it now, rather than look back to the good old days. Port is most evocative as a drink. It is the most traditional wine served at meals, yet probably the least understood. The difference between a sensational vintage or

The Douro Valley

old tawny port and a fresh ruby youngster is the difference between Château Lafite-Rothschild and red plonk. Sometimes the red plonk is served and fellow diners are expected to swoon with admiration. This is when the club closes ranks and says that all port is marvellous; it is then that the outside world need to judge by tasting and drinking the various qualities and draw their own conclusion.

I have been given unstinting help in my researches by my fellow port shippers and 'without them I would not be able to give the balanced view that I hope I have. A visit to the Douro Valley and to a port shipper's lodge in Vila Nova de Gaia enhances the quality of life.

In the meantime, there is a glossary at the end of the book for those peculiar aspects of port terminology.

The next time a bottle of port looks out in a rather embarrassed way on a retailer's shelf or a glass stands jauntily to the right, it is worth remembering that although much expertise has gone into the making of the wine, it is there first and foremost to be enjoyed. The port producers themselves in the Douro Valley and Vila Nova de Gaia will happily drink port as an aperitif either warm on a cold winter's morning or chilled by the swimming pool in the summer, in addition to the end of the meal. If port can tomorrow provoke as much discussion and evoke as much laughter as it has over the centuries, it can take us happily through the twenty-first century.

"The Prince Regent bumped his head when drinking a toast in a ship and declared that the Loyal Toast should be drunk sitting as soon as he became king."

Ernest Cockburn – Port Wine and Oporto.

I
Introduction

PORT IS PRODUCED in what must be one of the most inaccessible wine regions in the world; the Douro Valley in northern Portugal. No one would come across these vineyards by accident. The roads through and around them have been established during centuries of history; the countryside is wild, majestic and beautiful.

Produced in the 900-square-mile demarcated area of the Douro Valley and consumed in more than eighty countries, port is a wine which has had its fermentation arrested at the time of the vintage with grape alcohol, produced from distilled Portuguese table wine. This process produces a medium sweet fortified wine as some of the natural sugar content of the grape is retained.

The port shipper's art lies in the blending from a myriad of farmers' vineyards, using many different grape varieties, basking in several micro-climates that vary from year to year. It is this essential and critical labour of love that cannot be imitated elsewhere.

The "river of gold", as the Spanish word "Duero" and the Portuguese "Douro" signify, rises in Spain. It flows west, entering Portugal at Barca d'Alva and, twisting and turning through mountainous canyons flanked by vineyards, reaches the Atlantic Ocean at Oporto – a name that, in Portuguese, literally means "the port". The desolate, lonely area where port is produced is in 240,000 hectares on either side of the River Douro. Until recently, the river was the lifeline and the thoroughfare of the wine farmers – they had no other means of reaching the outside world. The *barcos rabelos*, which are single-sail boats that went up and down the river, had to be steered through dangerous rapids; farms could only be visited by walking or on horseback and over rough country. The pipes (casks each containing about 550 litres of wine) had to be lugged down to the river by ox carts and manhandled aboard. Nothing to do with port production has ever been easy.

But possibly the most astonishing thing about this king of fortified wines is that the region where it is made is totally unlike what most people would expect of a vineyard. First, there is no soil. The port vineyards thrive on schist, a term defined by the *Shorter Oxford Dictionary* as "a crystalline rock whose component minerals are arranged in a more or less parallel manner". The visitor, who risks stumbling if he or she walks uncertainly in the vineyards, might describe this schist as broken up pieces of slate-like rock, extremely hard and varying in size from lumps that are small boulders to chunks the size of the palm of one's hand. This schistous rock is, I maintain, port's secret – the reason for port being the wine it is. All wine regions have their own grape varieties, climates, even micro-climates, soils and contours, but nowhere else will you find the schist, which makes Portuguese grapes so hardy and tough. In former times in order to plant vines the schist had to be dynamited – one often used to hear the explosions when plantations were being established – but today, bulldozers are generally used. But no spade can turn this schist so that a vine can be set in it; remember, the tap root of a mature vine descends for at least twelve feet, and the mere fact that this plant is able to penetrate through the broken-up rock is itself something wonderful. Even when the vine is established, it has to fight for water throughout its life in this inhospitable area. The wine of these vines is unique – and no wonder.

The climate of the port region of the upper Douro ranges from ferocious heat in the summer – over 40°C is not unusual – to below freezing in the winter. It is hard country. The towns are scattered and villages are few and far between. The peasants are true people of their soil or, rather, of the schist and of the weather conditions, and they can be as generous and hospitable as they can be tough and obdurate. The rainfall is half that of Oporto, around 50cm (20 inches) per year.

Port has two birthplaces; the upper Douro vineyards and the "lodges" (lojas) in Vila Nova de Gaia, literally "Gaia New Town", which is the main suburb of Oporto, across the swirling Douro from that city. Oporto proper is to the north, Vila Nova de

Gaia to the south, and, by law, all shippers have to have their offices and lodges, where they mature their wines, in this area. As Gaia is built on a hill, all roads lead to the river. Twisting cobbled streets and lanes separate the lodges, some being on the river bank, others higher, with spectacular views over the Douro and Oporto. In this comparatively compact area the fifty-five registered port shippers mature the equivalent of 250 million bottles of port, all in large vats or pipes. The long, narrow lodges are at ground level, sheltered by red-tiled roofs, supported by pillars and beams that were often put in place hundreds of years ago. As a result of mergers and take-overs, these companies have now regrouped into a total of twenty-nine different firms. Even so, for any port shipper, his friendliest rival (and, in the port trade, rivalry can indeed be friendly) or his bitterest competitor will only be at work a few hundred yards away.

The climate in Gaia is rather different from that of the port vineyards. It can still be very hot in the summer, but the proximity to the Atlantic can make it very cold and wet in the winter; morning sea fogs and high humidity are commonplace. It is this atmosphere of Gaia which traditionally has been a major contributory force in port production. Not only does the wine mature to perfection – the humidity protracts its progress instead of too great heat drying it up and causing serious losses due to excess of evaporation – but the shippers, in their lodges, are able to undertake the complex processes of blending in conditions that are ideal, especially for wines that are destined to be drunk in northern countries, where port has always been loved. The rich fullness of port helps shut out the cold.

The light, too, in Gaia is different from that further up the Douro. This is of great importance with a wine where the colour is one of its great beauties and where hours of time and generations of experience contribute to composing the famous rubies and tawnies.

The port shippers tend either to live in the residential district of Foz do Douro to the west of Oporto, or somewhere around within easy driving distance of their offices. It is an odd day when a shipper does not meet one of his own kind going to the office, although a cheery wave or friendly grin is more likely to be an initial "thank you" for last night's dinner than any acquiescence of market share stakes.

Vila Nova de Gaia was originally chosen to be the entrepôt (entreposto) of the port trade because the pipes of port coming down the Douro on the graceful "barcos rabelos" could be easily off-loaded on to the quays, taken up and down the lanes by ox-cart and be shipped over the "bar", the mouth of the river, to all overseas markets. Nowadays the port arrives from the Douro Valley in tanker lorries, and the winding roads and steep hills of Gaia are wholly unsuitable for both tankers and TIR lorries alike. Nearly all port now is shipped in containers, not from Oporto, but from the purpose-built port of Leixões, ten kilometres north of Oporto. The entrepôt of Vila Nova de Gaia is thus outdated. However, all port shippers' offices have still by law to be in the entrepôt, which is pleasing traditionally although frustrating commercially.

II
The History of Port

No wine is more inextricably linked to its country of origin than port. It is even included in the name of the country itself. The history, as it relates to this guide, starts with Romans. They crossed the River Douro from the north in 137 BC, invading the Celtic inhabitants of Portugal, or Lusitania as it was then called. The land they saw must have been totally unsuitable for their agricultural needs and, in order to grow crops, they had to build terraces, thus laying the foundation of the vineyards that we have today. They could not do without wine and so they set about planting vines as well as cereals.

However, the Romans were not the only ones to cross the Pyrenees. During the Dark Ages of the first century several barbarian tribes came in, intent on the sun and the easy living it provided. One of these, the Swabians, who were good horsemen, journeyed into the Douro Valley and found the local wine tempting enough for them to stay. They in turn spent the next four hundred years keeping at bay the Visigoths, who were trying to expand their kingdom northwards up the Iberian Peninsula. A bored faction seeking peace decided to invite the Moors from North Africa to cross the Straits of Gibraltar and, with alacrity, these captured the treasure of the Visigothic Kings and reached the Douro from the south in 716. But the Moors were essentially southern peoples. They did not appreciate "this ignorant country where naught is heard but the sound of tempests" (St Fructuosus, Bishop of Braga in the seventh century) and they gradually withdrew from northern Portugal, leaving behind a few Moorish castles in Numão and Lavandeira.

This territory, the land between the rivers Minho and Douro, then called the Territora Portucalense, later the County of Portugal, became the nucleus of the Portuguese kingdom.

Every student and lover of wine wants a point from which to date when a particular classic wine actually started to be cultivated and why in any one area. After the inevitable Romans, the first important date for Portuguese viticulture is 1095.

Two years before, in 1093, a young French adventurer, Count Henry of Burgundy, married Teresa, the illegitimate daughter of King Alfonso VI of Castile and León; the king threw in the then obscure County of Portugal as part of the dowry. The count, being a cousin of the powerful Duke of Burgundy, was partial to the sword and the grape. It is said that the native Galician wines were too thin for his robust taste and that he became homesick for the rich, strong wines of his home country; so he imported cuttings of the Pinot Noir grape variety from Burgundy into Portugal, hoping to produce fuller wines. The Portuguese, with diluted chauvinism, soon renamed this the Tinta Francisca. Today, the Tinta Francisca is still one of the dominant grape varieties used in the Douro Valley.

So the marriage of Portugal and wine had really begun and ironically the marriage of Henry and Teresa provided the founder of the Portuguese kingdom. Their one son, Alfonso Henriques, born in 1109, was a noisy, ambitious youth and by the time he had come of age, his father having already died, mother and son were locked in battle for control of the country. Son defeated mother at São Mamende and, after brushing with his cousin Alfonso, continued his expansion south to take in the land from Viana do Castelo in the north to Coimbra in the south, and eastwards almost to the modern frontier between Portugal and Spain. During this time, Alfonso progressively ennobled himself from count to duke, from duke to prince and, finally, to king.

Aided and abetted by various Anglo-Norman, Flemish and German Crusaders over the next half century, King Alfonso I saw his originally tiny country grow to embrace most of present-day Portugal. The new kingdom received official recognition in 1178 when Pope Alexander III confirmed Alfonso in his conquests and recognized the rights of his successors. The final conquest of the Algarve was achieved by his grandson, King Alfonso III, in 1249, when Faro capitulated.

The thirteenth and fourteenth centuries heralded the beginnings of sea trading; merchant venturers from Italy and England converged on Lisbon, merchants from Genoa and Lombardy brought spices overland from the East and the English wool merchants traded cloth and corn for wine and olive oil. Six thousand casks of wine were exported annually. Such was the extent of trading with England that in 1353 the merchants of Lisbon and Oporto made their own commercial treaty with Edward III. This allowed the Portuguese to fish cod, then, as now, their staple dish and national pride – bacalhau – off the English coast in return for regular shipments of wine sent in small casks from Viana in the north. Thus the "English Connection" was forged. This treaty was the forerunner of the Anglo-Portuguese Treaty of Windsor – a pact of perpetual friendship, which was ratified in May 1386 in the Star Chamber at Westminster. This formed the basis of England's oldest foreign alliance and encompassed political, military, and commercial matters; the subjects of both countries were granted the right to trade in either country on the terms enjoyed by the nationals of that country; freedom of travel was guaranteed.

It was this friendly feeling between these early merchants more than six hundred years ago that truly laid the foundation stone for the discovery, enjoyment, expansion and continuity of Portuguese wine, port, the port shippers and the port trade as we know it today. Many elements have intervened, some not always advantageous, during the years, but the commercial sturdiness of those bygone days exemplifies the spirit of friendly conviviality that is associated with port, that most robust, round and full of all fortified wines.

The Anglo-Portuguese link was further strengthened, and indeed ennobled, when John of Gaunt, Duke of Lancaster and uncle of King Richard II, managed to persuade King João I of Portugal (1385– 1433) to marry his daughter Philippa. (Students of English literature will not need reminding that in the Lancaster household there was employed the son of a vintner, who certainly knew something about wine – Geoffrey Chaucer.) The match took some time to arrange, as the king seemed in no great hurry to forsake his bachelorhood but, finally, the wedding was celebrated in Oporto with due ceremony; the couple, clad in cloth of gold and wearing golden crowns, rode on white horses through the town to the cathedral. A festive wedding banquet followed in the bishop's palace which, in turn, gave way to dancing and singing until the bride and bridegroom were allowed to go to bed alone in the royal bed-chamber. They seem to have been happy and their fifth child, Prince Henry, born in 1394, was later immortalized in history books as Henry the Navigator. He, no doubt aware of the advantages of trade as a means to a very prosperous end, decided that it was about time that the Portuguese set sail and explored the world, rather than always playing host to exploring venturers. He tirelessly financed and organized voyages that opened up the horizons of Africa, Brazil, India and the East Indies. The English and Portuguese courts became very close and, taking advantage of the Anglo-French wars, the wines of Portugal began to replace the increasingly scarce wines of France in the English market. But it was not yet port as we know it today that was finding its way to taverns and dining rooms up and down England; the wine from Portugal that was being exported came mainly from the Minho in the north of the country. It was usually astringent and light, was shipped through the port of Viana de Castelo and was consumed as "Red Portugal" wine.

In these embryonic commercial days, the wine trade probably continued to develop along the lines of barter; cloth and cod for "Red Portugal". Such was the impetus of this increasingly and mutually successful trade that English merchants gradually decided to settle and establish themselves in Viana de Castelo and Moncão. They were able to control their trade better *in situ*. It is a remarkable tribute to both nations that trade established six hundred years ago should prove such a firm base of trust and friendship, that neither country has fought the other during this very long period. It may be a case of both countries being seafaring nations jointly facing the Atlantic; but, whatever the reason, it is a marvellous pledge of the mutual enjoyment that wine can bring.

Moving to and working in Portugal then must have been similar to establishing a company now in a producing country where you believe the prospects and potential to be worthwhile. Indeed, during Elizabeth I's reign, in 1578, an English consul was even appointed in Viana to protect English interests. The merchants, or "factors" as they were then called, began to explore inland in search of better quality wines. They moved south-east into the Douro Valley proper. Here, because of the superior quality of the soil, they found that their vines produced fuller and harder wine. They liked what they saw. They also realized that this could well be a new solid base to build up and capitalize on this new successful two-way trade, as their trading cousins in England had increased the size of their fishing fleet and perfected a new art in the curing of cod, which was in great demand by the Portuguese.

All this was taking place against the background of what is referred to as the "captivity" when, for sixty years following Philip II of Spain's annexation of the Portuguese crown in 1580, Portugal was ruled as a Spanish province from Madrid. This was the era of the Armada and Drake and the Spanish Inquisition. The yearned-for independence did not occur until 1640, when Portugal re-emerged as an independent state in Europe. Although peace was signed between Spain and England in 1604, it was not until the Favoured Nation Treaty in 1654, signed between Cromwell and King John IV, that Anglo-Portuguese trade once again became officially immune from political and military ravages. John IV's daughter, Catherine of Braganza, further strengthened the ties between the two countries when she married King Charles II of England.

Because the vines in the Douro Valley yielded better wine, the English factors began to move from Viana and establish themselves in Oporto. They could ship the wine down the River Douro, thus forsaking their old port of Viana. Together with their southern counterparts in Lisbon, these English factors formed a colony with their own consuls, judges, rules of society and religion.

The port trade was gradually evolving, through helpful outside circumstances. The protectionist policies pursued by Louis XIV through his minister Colbert led to England imposing heavy additional duties on French wines. Then, in turn, when English cloth was forbidden to be imported into France, Charles II decided to prohibit French wines altogether from coming into England. Although claret was then the Englishman's favourite wine, because England and France were constantly at war it was now considered an unpatriotic drink. Jacobites continued to drink it surreptitiously, as they did later as a sign of their adherence to the Stuart King "over the water" after 1688, but loyal Whigs toasted the king in tankards of red port. Italian wines, previously introduced to the English palate through the Grand Tours of Europe of that era, were at this time lacking in quality and quantity, so the shortage of red wine in England gave ample scope for even more sales of red wine from

Portugal.

1678 saw the first officially recorded shipment of "Vinho do Porto" registered in the Oporto customs. The total that year was 408 pipes; twenty-five years later, in 1693, total shipments had expanded to 13,011 pipes. Ironically, also in 1678, two younger sons were despatched from England to Portugal to learn the trade and find wines that were of the top quality for English gentlemen. They are never named, but in all books on port the story goes that, on their way to the Douro Valley, they stayed in a monastery in Lamego. The abbot, a kindly and generous host, gave the travellers his best wine, from Pinhão. The two brothers were intrigued and delighted at what they tasted, they had never experienced anything like it before. The abbot, who obviously had a sweet tooth, explained that he had added several litres of local brandy to the cask during fermentation, thus conserving the natural sugar of the grape.

The brothers so liked this rounder, smoother, sweeter wine that they decided to import this style back home. But although other producers were already adding brandy after fermentation to stabilise wine for its journey to England, it was not for another fifty years that it became the accepted practice to add brandy to arrest the fermentation. Coincidentally or not, it was just about this time that another man of God, Dom Pérignon, was changing drinking history by creating a sparkling wine which all the world knows as Champagne.

This is the right place to consider what an extraordinary resilient life-cycle port – both the wine and the trade – enjoys. It is interesting to note that amongst the factors who had already settled in Oporto by 1700 were three families, whose companies, even today, are still to the forefront of the port trade: Croft, Taylor and Warre are the descendant companies of these original families. In those days it was customary for the firms to change names, depending on who the partners were: thus, Phayre and Bradley, formed in 1678, became Tilden, Thompson and Croft, then Thompson, Croft and Mitchell in 1742, Croft, Stewart and Croft in 1759, Thompson, Croft & Co. in 1769, and thereafter, Croft & Co. up to the present day. To become a partner in a leading firm of port shippers was both as socially acceptable and financially profitable as becoming a lawyer. Sande-man's have kept the notion alive by continuing to sell their "Partners

Port", an old, full port, based on a blend originally created in 1890 for the then partners, Albert, Ernest and Walter Sandeman.

It is not only impossible but would render this historical sketch meaningless, if I attempted to ignore the famous British port firms that are such an integral part of the enjoyment of port. The fact is that they invented it, were the first to export it, intermarried because of it and are still, over three hundred years later, the trustees of it throughout the world. The sheer age of these companies is awe-inspiring. I remember talking to some Americans, explaining that Croft, then celebrating its tercentenary, was founded in 1678. They could not believe it – "But that's a hundred years before our whole country was founded!"

The following two and a half centuries after the Methuen Treaty in 1703 help explain the slow moving pace and stubborness of the descendants of these early settlers. By nature these men were tough and ambitious; they had to be. They were pioneers, and what they were pioneering was wild, desolate, mountainous, unpleasant and often dangerous country. Today, the Douro Valley is still wild, desolate and mountainous, but no longer unpleasant or dangerous for the traveller but it is rough country where boots are needed and mosquitos unhappily abound.

Englishmen were predominant in these early days of the port wine trade, although the Dutch and Germans were also represented by such well-known families as the Kopkes, Burmester and the Van Zellers.

The Methuen Treaty of 1703 enabled Portuguese wines to be imported into England at one third less duty than that imposed on French wines. In return for this, English woollen cloth was to be admitted to Portugal free of duty. This treaty was the start for the equivalent of the gold rush in the Douro Valley.

> *Be sometimes to your country true.*
> *Have once the public good in mind.*
> *Bravely despise Champagne at court.*
> *And choose to dine at home with port.*

wrote Swift, urging Britons to eschew French wines.

Port continued its patriotic path. As the irrepressible Dr Samuel Johnson summed up "Claret is the liquor for boys: port for men".

He, like many other great Englishmen, was a three bottle a day man; another was the extraordinary squire, eccentric John Mytton, who boasted that he broached his first bottle of port each day "whilst shaving". (Although port bottles were not then the size they are today and the wine was not as high in alcohol. John Croft, who wrote the all-embracing work *Treatise on the wines of Portugal* in 1788, stipulates that

> An Englishman of any decent condition or circumstances, cannot dispense with it after his good dinner, in the same way as he uses a piece of Cheshire cheese for pretended digestion's sake.

In order to keep up this demand for quality and tradition, changes had to take place back in the Douro Valley. More planting of vines was necessary; farmers who had previously eked out a living from corn and wheat, became vineyard owners overnight. Inevitably, the Church became large property owners and tended to make better wine than the recently converted farmers; John Croft claimed "their wine fetched a higher price, was stouter and stronger than common, and was very fashionable in England where it went by the name of 'Priest Port' ".

It is difficult, though many have tried, to pinpoint exactly when port crossed the line from being a tough and rather harsh table wine from the Douro, to being the fruity and smooth fortified wine from the Douro that we enjoy today. We know that it was gently fortified to stabilize it during its sea voyage, thus keeping it in good condition. But apart from the good abbot in Lamego, it would appear that some firms used some local brandy to arrest the fermentation only some of the time and it seems unlikely that all firms used grape spirit in uniform proportions until around 1850.

The second consideration was to control the standard of quality and quantity of port. Inevitably where demand exceeds supply there are those who cut corners and raise prices and others who have a vested interest in doing the opposite. The farmers, intent on producing all that was required of them during these boom years, started to fatten up the poor vintages which produced light wines with the juice of the elderberry, "baga". As makers of home-made country wines will know, this fruit contributes a beautiful deep colour and smooth flavour to beverages. So in 1727 the British wine shippers in Oporto formed themselves into an Association, whose main objective was to control the quality of the wine, to satisfy their customers in England.

Apart from our inventive abbot at Lamego back in 1678, the flourishing port trade was a prime and classic example of English venturism, but soon the Portuguese realized that they must do something about this profitable sector trading right under their noses.

The Marquês de Pombal, 1699–1782, formerly Sebastião José de Carvalho e Melo, now the autocratic prime minister of King Joseph I (1750–1777), was such a man to intervene. The English, through their Factory (where factors met, not where wine was made, see page 101) in Oporto, were still complaining about poor quality and the adulteration that some farmers were practising. The farmers sent a deputation to Lisbon and Pombal, fresh from having restored the capital from a disastrous earthquake, in which twenty thousand people were killed, acted straight away. In 1756 he did two things which implemented and changed the history of the port trade: he established the world's first demarcated wine region by confirming nature's gifts in law, and he established the Royal Oporto Wine Company which now took on the sole right to distill grape brandy with which to fortify the wines and controlled all grape prices. Naturally, the British, hitherto unchallenged, were indignant at this monopoly. Gradually they learnt to live with it, as after all the quality did improve, presumably as a result of cleaner production methods and the use of neutral grape spirit, and the port trade was becoming an established, as well as being a most acceptable, way of life. The English and Portuguese needed each other. As John Croft said towards the end of the eighteenth century, "a shipper's business needed substantial capital firstly, because the wines cost more to purchase and secondly, because the shipper was obliged to keep his wines on hand for a considerable time due to the fashion for the oldest wines then prevalent in England".

Light was thus dawning that wine improved with age. To keep wine in casks in England was not very convenient; at this stage, bottles were squat and bulbous, designed solely for transporting the wine drawn from the cask to the table. As these bottles could not be stowed away on their sides the wine was unable to be in contact with the cork and therefore oxidized. But lateral thinking (literally) took over and by 1775 the bottle, with a longer body and shorter neck, had been sufficiently elongated to be binned. That year, says Warner Allen, Oporto produced "the first wine which could worthily claim the title of vintage port". It was probably the world's first vintage wine, for the first bottled vintage claret did not appear until 1787, at Château Lafite.

The port trade expanded, so much so that it is recorded in 1792 that 50,000 pipes (nearly thirty-six million bottles) were shipped to Britain. That is a lot of port. In fact it is three times as much as is shipped to the U.K. today, to a much larger population than then existed. Our "three bottle a day" ancestors were mighty men, worthy customers of the intrepid merchants of the Douro. .

The British factors would receive orders from their principals in Britain to buy certain quantities of port up to a certain price, which instructions they did their best to follow; they then drew for the amount of the invoice through their bankers. In the invoices the cost of staves and iron hoops was charged. Interestingly, the pipes were first made by British coopers, recruited from various breweries and sent out to Oporto, who then initiated the Portuguese into their art, with the results that the Portuguese coopers became some of the finest exponents of their crafts in the world. Look up at the beams in the roof of some of the older lodges to see what masters they were – and are. In 1788 a tax was imposed on every pipe of port shipped for the purposes of financing a road-making scheme; it showed that the wealthy merchants could afford to contribute towards social benefits.

Around this time the merchants decided to consolidate their trading and social position in Oporto, by building for themselves a Factors' House in the Rua Nova dos Ingleses. They had met informally in the street to discuss trading matters for a number of years. What a marvellous sight it must have been, the gentlemen wearing top hats and carrying malacca canes, sporting fine waistcoats and gloves, all standing in the cobbled street, discussing trade. They then retired into their residential club. Happily, this sight was recorded for posterity in a marvellously detailed painting by J. J. Forrester in 1834, which shows the leading English and Portuguese merchants chatting and strolling on the Rua Nova dos Ingleses. It must have been a glorious cross between the floor of a Stock Exchange and a country house fair.

However, it was decided to pull this club down to make way for a magnificent building, universally known as the Factory House. A most attractive personality, John Whitehead, was the then British Consul who supervised the construction of this imposing granite building, which still today acts as the cornerstone of the port trade. (See page 101). Whitehead was Consul for forty-six years and was a skilled mathematician, architect, bibliophile and scientist, a pillar of the Oporto British establishment.

As John Delaforce points out in his recent book *The Factory House at Oporto*, the difference between the British Factory and the Factory House is that the former was the name given to British merchants or "factors" collectively, whereas the latter is the name given to the actual building used by them as their headquarters. In turn, the Factory House has been the headquarters of the British Association, composed of British port wine shippers, with their partners and directors as individual members, since 1814. The British Association became the legal owner of the Factory House some time after December 1848 when the purchase price of the freehold was paid.

The building of the Factory House provided an excellent introduction to the nineteenth century, for this was the most eventful and progressive period for port. The French Revolution in 1789 had again caused the sale of French wines to decline in England. Oporto changed hands twice during the Peninsular War; the French under Marshal Soult captured the city in March 1809; two months later it was retaken by the future Duke of Wellington, then Sir Arthur Wellesley. Against a background of sieges, civil war and revolution that characterized the early part of the century, and then the dreadful phylloxera, wending its way southward from France, that caused havoc in the vineyards from 1868–1885, certain characters stepped onto the stage who personified the resilience of the port trade. They helped shape the trade to withstand the ravages of political intervention, thus maintaining a stability of trading. They and the great vintage ports, such as 1815 (always known as "Waterloo"), 1834, 1847, 1863 and 1896 helped create an aura that the port trade has never lost.

Joseph James Forrester was the first, and possibly the greatest of these characters, because he was talented in so many different ways. Born in Hull in 1809, he came to Oporto in 1831 to join his uncle in

(125)

Burnt mark
'T' x C

N & B *10 Pipes.*

SHIPPED, by the Grace of God, in good Order, and well conditioned *Croft & Co.* in and upon the good Ship called the *Mary* whereof is Master, under God, for this present Voyage, *Jacob Tindall* and now riding at Anchor in the River DOURO, and by God's Grace bound *London, with or without Convoy* to say

Ten Pipes Red Port Wine ——,

being marked and numbered as in the Margin, and are to be delivered in the like Order and well conditioned, at the aforesaid Port of *London* (all and every the Dangers and Accidents of the Seas and Navigation, of what Nature or kind and howsoever occasioned excepted) unto *Messrs Noble*

Bills or to their Assigns, he or they paying Freight for the said *Four Pounds Sterling per Ten of two Pipes without Convoy, and if with Six Pounds.* —— with Primage and Average accustomed. In Witness whereof the Master, or Purser the said Ship hath affirmed to four Bills of Lading, all of this Tenor and Date one of which four Bills being accomplished, the other three to stand void. And God send the good Ship to her desir'd Port in Safety. Amen. Dated in PORT

June 1815. ——

Jacob Tindall

✓

Document recording a shipment of port from Croft, approximately coinciding with the end of the Battle of Waterloo.

the already established wine firm of Offley, Webber and Forrester. He was not given to accepting the rigid code of Englishness that had already grown up in the community and immediately began to learn to speak Portuguese fluently. This in itself was unusual.

Forrester delved into every detail of the port trade, travelled extensively in the Douro Valley and, being artistically minded and a skilled cartographer, produced definitive maps of Oporto, the wine region, the Douro bed showing the rapids and geological formations, wine diseases and so on. The maps are not only remarkable for their accuracy – they are works of art. He also illustrated essays on olive oil, vegetables, cereals and fruits in the Douro and made a collection of earthenware figures representing each village's costume of the period. His watercolours show an uncanny grasp of reality blended with creative genius. In the wine world he was determined to see fair play; it was his nature. In 1844, aged only thirty-five he wrote a pamphlet *"A word or two on Port Wine"* in which he alleged that certain trade malpractices were lowering the standards of port. Uproar from the English community; gradual calmness. Purist that he was, Forrester believed that port should be a natural wine, that is to say, he believed that the addition of brandy to arrest the fermentation was not correct. Fortunately in this one instance he was overruled, for if this brilliant and likeable man had had his way, then port would have continued to be thin – Burgundian in style and not the great dessert wine it is today. From the nineteenth century, therefore, our three-bottle-a-day men recede into the shadows.

Forrester had immense charm. In 1847 he achieved the singular feat of entertaining the leaders of both sides of a revolt to dinner at the same time in different rooms in his house at Oporto. He was created Barão (Baron) de Forrester by the king of Portugal and given many other decorations by the emperors of Russia, Austria and France and by Pope Pius IX.

Other names that have since become interwoven with the circulation of the decanters include Cabel Roope, who, at the races, was once asked by King Carlos I (1890–1908) whether he had a horse in the next race. Roope replied in his excruciating Portuguese, "Sir, teno uma cavala muito beng thought-of"; which actually meant "Sir, I have a very well thought-of mackerel" (the Portuguese for horse is "cavalo", not "cavala"). Indeed, up until quite recently many of the British shippers spoke truly fractured Portuguese, rather as pre-Revolution Russians of good birth spoke Russian with an accent. But today things are different – Robin Reid of Croft speaks a particularly pure Portuguese – just as Fernando van Zeller of Noval or Fernando de Almeida of Ferreira speak beautiful and idiomatic English.

There was Arthur Dagge, who broke etiquette and married a washerwoman from the desolate village of Mogadouro; Albert George Sandeman, who became the hundredth governor of the Bank of England and whose brother, Colonel John Glas Sandeman, invented the "Penny-in-the-slot" machine with the aid of a merchant called Everitt.

Perhaps the most dedicated of the nineteenth-century personalities of port was neither English nor a man. Dona Antonia Adelaide Ferreira, born in 1810 at Regua, lived her entire life in the world of port until her death in 1896. She ruled her estates with a kindly rod of iron, having first married her cousin, then her manager. "There were never two men who spent more money in the Douro than the two husbands of Dona Antonia," commented Charles Sellers. Her achievements would be remarkable at any time – in the nineteenth century and in what is still predominantly a masculine world, they are heroic. And she inaugurated a tradition of fine winemaking.

The dreaded phylloxera, the plant louse that had already ravaged much of France's vineyards, struck the Douro in 1868. Immediately, production was down fifty per cent on the previous year. There seemed no cure. The 1881, although declared by most shippers, could have been an outstanding year both in quantity and quality, but tiny quantities were made. I remember a Morgan 1881 that I tasted exactly a hundred years later; it was delicious, still fruity, but disappeared fast. However, the American root stock, found to be resistant to the phylloxera, was gradually introduced to the vineyards, the national vines were grafted onto this and the port shippers breathed again.

The port trade also endured devastations such as the cholera epidemic in 1899 and intermittent fearful floods; one such was in 1909, which wreaked havoc in the lodges and resulted in much loss of wine. World War I, like all wars, naturally restricted shipments of port, but the Anglo-Portuguese commercial treaties of 1914 and 1916 established the legal definition of port, and made it mandatory for a certificate of origin to accompany all shipments.

By this time, all the great shippers had established themselves in Oporto. There were twenty British firms in a community of fifty British families. Annual shipments towards the turn of the century were around 89,000 pipes; Great Britain took the lion's share, but exports already were finding their way to the U.S., Europe, Australia, Russia and the Far East. Port shippers started to buy quintas in the Douro so that they could use these farmhouses as a base at vintage time; they had their own beach at Foz (the residential suburb of Oporto), they played golf at Espinho, cricket in Oporto (see page 104), went partridge shooting at vintage time and shot snipe in the marshes in Aveiro. A few years ago in Aveiro I tried the latter sport with Robin Reid, happily an expert shot; the calmness of the marshes was marvellous, the sunset exquisite, the bottle of old tawny port I was sharing was beautiful – but could I shoot one snipe . . . no.

The years immediately after World War I were to be port's really prosperous period. More port than ever before or since was shipped out of Oporto in 1925 – we still have not caught up with the volume that was being consumed then! In the mid-1920s, port was in fashion; the cocktail party had not yet crossed the Atlantic. Annual shipments were up to 95,000 pipes, almost seventy million bottles. The fact was that, through long association, people in Britain thoroughly enjoyed drinking this sweet red wine; the preference was there and, as Britain was still somewhat class conscious, there evolved two quite separate markets for port: one was the preserve of the dinner party, the other was the much wider preserve of the pub. "Port and lemon" (lemonade – the fizzy sort) accounted for eighty per cent of total consumption during this time and was the favoured drink in pub bars before Babycham took this market.

The Wall Street crash in 1929 and the ensuing world slump inevitably hit the port trade as all others. The Portuguese government took this opportunity to redefine and reorganize their port trade so as to control the vagaries of it better. In 1933 they established three main bodies to supervise the trade; the Instituto do Vinho do Porto (the Port Wine Institute), the Casa do Douro (the Farmers and Wine Growers Association) and the Gremio dos Exportadores do Vinho do Porto (the Port Wine Shippers Association). The Instituto do Vinho do Porto is the official government body which controls the other two (see page 105).

By 1936 the port trade had climbed back to nearly sixty million bottles. The ending of prohibition in the U.S.A. had opened up that huge market. It is recorded that, such was the wish to satisfy long-denied thirsty throats, one port company was able to ship twenty thousand cases to their customer only two and a half days after the arrival of the port in cask from Oporto. Such efficiency would be hard to match today.

France had already become a steady customer for port and in 1936 imported over 500,000 bottles. Owing to the high duty in the U.K., it was at this time that port was allowed by the Customs and Excise Board to be bottled under bond. This meant that bottling became more centralized as the suppliers, instead of a myriad of wine merchants, could now bottle port under Customs and Excise supervision and duty did not have to be paid until the port was cleared from bond.

However, World War II virtually brought the port trade to a standstill. Port was considered a luxury item in Britain and therefore was on quota. Supplies were restricted to how much each shipper could allow to merchants who might previously have ordered as much as they thought they might require. Even by the mid-1950s, the port market was only able to reclaim half the consumption they had enjoyed before the war. It was not until 1963 that port sales started to climb back up again through the forty million bottle mark. This year was when, for the first time, France overtook Britain as the leading importer of port. Port thus stopped being "the Englishman's wine" in 1963, and the French have never looked back.

The strength of the U.K. breweries and wine merchants was no match for the baffled port shippers. Except for the Sandeman range and Gilbey's Triple Crown (supplied by Croft), the other port-shippers had not developed their brands. They still happily supplied port in bulk to the brewers and the wine merchants, who put their own labels on these bottles of ruby and tawny port. They would change suppliers for a mere ten shillings a pipe during the early 1960s.

The port shippers saw France as being a valuable alternative market. In turn, the French were able to buy good quality drier blends which led to port being a very acceptable and accepted aperitif. "*Un verre de porto*" became the snob imported aperitif before the French discovered whisky. As we in Britain would offer a glass of sherry to a guest at home, the French would offer a glass of port. Sherry is still almost unknown in France, whereas by the end of the 1970s France was consuming forty per cent of all port exports at the rate of thirty million bottles a year. The same amount as total exports to all world markets just twenty years earlier.

The 1970s not only saw the supremacy of France as the leading port-consuming nation; this decade saw enormous changes in the direction of the port trade. More and more port shippers began bottling ports under their own label instead of shipping it in bulk and allowing their customers to put on their own private labels. In turn, this led to more port being bottled in Portugal. In 1970, only 12 per cent of all exports were bottled by the shippers themselves in Vila

Nova de Gaia; ten years later, this proportion had risen to nearly 50 per cent. Greater quality control could be exercised and international brands began to be developed.

III
Vineyards and Vines

The landscape

UNLESS YOU HIRE a private helicopter, the vineyards are still today three hours' travelling time away from the offices and lodges of the port shippers, as they have been for the last hundred years. Whether you go by train, bus or car, three hours must elapse between the time you leave Oporto to the time you reach the main centres of the Douro Valley at Regua or Pinhão.

The Douro Valley is the demarcated region where port must be produced. The River Douro rises in Spain, where it is known as the Duero, and winds down through the snow-capped peaks of the Sierra de Urbión, pushing westwards past Vallodolid until it serves as the Spanish/Portuguese frontier. For the remaining one-third of its length, it flows, sometimes gently, sometimes tumultuously, through northern Portugal to Oporto.

The Douro district as defined by Portuguese law is the area starting forty-five miles east of Oporto up to the Spanish frontier. It stretches for about forty miles west to east and ten to thirty miles north to south. The deep gorges and beautiful scenery form the most remarkable and unlikely birthplace for port. This is the Douro Valley, wild, majestic, tough and lonely. Yet, like New York, if you know someone it can be friendly, fun and very hospitable. It is, without doubt, the most amazing region to be known throughout the world as the home of a smooth, round, fruity wine. The countryside is so hard and unyielding, freezing in winter and boiling in summer. Yet here is heaven for the port lover. The terraced vineyards rise steeply from the River Douro and its tributaries and girdle the hills and even the mountains. They are dotted with houses and olive trees, a real tribute to man's perseverance in this once desolate landscape.

It is utterly remote from the industrial town of Oporto and its cousin Vila Nova de Gaia, south across the river. Here in the entreposto, up cobbled streets and often jammed together in awkward spaces, are the lodges and offices of the port-shippers. Their life is totally different from that of the Douro farmer; they are still able to enjoy a life style that is both urban and urbane – the town versus the country at its toughest. Both sets of men respect each other, but whether they really understand each other is debatable.

Nevertheless, it is the port shippers who take over the responsibility of the farmers' wine. They organize its transport from the Douro Valley to Vila Nova de Gaia, they accommodate the wine in their casks and mature it in their lodges. They are also responsible for selling it to port drinkers around the world, promoting it in countries where it is already known, opening up new markets everywhere. The two component and interlinking parts of port, the vineyards and the wine, are thus geographically and psychologically split.

The vineyards

I have long held the view that the secret of port is schist soil. Schist, from the Greek *schistos*, meaning "divided", is defined as "a geological term applied to rocks which have a foliated structure and split in thin irregular plates" (see also p. 2). There is little other. Indeed, the first-time visitor may query the use of the term "soil" for the loose plaques of stony substance, some like hard gravel, others like huge slates, seem quite unrelated to earth in which plants can be grown. Stout shoes or boots are needed for walking as the schist will score or cut all but the toughest soles and anyone with weak ankles is advised to take a stick.

Until the advent of bulldozers as recently as ten years ago, vines could be planted only after the schistous rocks had been blasted with dynamite, which is still often used – and heard. Sticks of dynamite are placed in the appropriate place, the holes covered with branches to reduce the effects of the explosion, the fuse is lit, the labourers run for cover behind another rock, the blast occurs and the planting can begin.

In the offices of the Real Companhia, which is the important successor to the State Company created by Marquês de Pombal in 1756, I saw the original map of the Douro Valley, before Baron Forrester's remarkable classic maps in the nineteenth century gave a new dimension to Douro cartography. This early map shows the Douro Valley, not in the correct east-west axis, but rather on a north-south axis, like a tree; it is beautifully sketched, faded but still clear to read. The interesting aspect of it is that in the eighteenth century the wine-producing region only extended eastwards as far as São João da Pesqueira. This was because the Cachão da Valeira, close by, marked the upper limit of navigation as there was an enormous rock blocking the gorge. The river was the vein of life and virtually everything and everyone travelled by it.

It took twelve years to break down and finally remove this rocky barrier and from then on it was possible to cultivate the area leading up to the Spanish frontier. But up until that time the wine-producing region was classified into 105 areas and São João da Pesqueira was the 105th. The wine region stopped at this point because the railway, completed in 1870, also stopped here. The map marks the outer limits of the Douro Valley. These were later clarified by highlighting the schist areas around the river and excluding the granite outcrops and that land which was above 1500 feet.

The incredible steepness of the terrain (you have to be very fit to run up the steps that connect terraces in a port vineyard) made it mandatory for narrow terraces, often just wide enough for one row of vines, to be built whenever more vines were needed. The terraces hold the schist around the vines and the walls prevent the bitter winds and winter rains from sweeping it downhill. All built by hand, the terraced walls curving around the contours of the Douro Valley stand as a lasting monument to hard, dignified labour over several centuries. Once there was the time and the willingness to spend hour upon hour in the furnace-like summer or bleak winter to ensure that the flow of the precious nectar should continue. Generations of peasant farmers, untried and uninterested in the outside world, followed their crop pattern unerringly year after year. Their relationship with the port shippers, who came regularly to the vineyards on horseback or by boat, must have been strange; the merchants must be admired for their toughness, courage and competence and the farmers respected for the way in which they continued to keep going and supply the wine, often with no other form of contract than a word and a handshake. Even today, there are long-established associations of this sort.

Phylloxera

Phylloxera vastatrix, an aphis that attacks the base of the vine, established itself in the port vineyards in the 1870s. It was in 1863 that a cluster of unknown insects was discovered on a vine in a greenhouse in Hammersmith, London. During the same year, vineyards in the Rhône Valley were similarly attacked and then all the vineyards of France. Five years later the plague had crossed the Pyrenees and Spain and was into Portugal.

The effect of Phylloxera was that during the spring, the green leaves lost their normal colour, turned yellow, then red, dark red, and by the end of August had all shrivelled up and fallen off. Some grapes survived through to the vintage, but were acid and watery. During the pruning time in December, the vines that had survived were dry and brittle. The full effect of this disease sometimes took up to three years, but by then the vine was certainly and irrevocably dead. When the roots were dug up, they were black and rotting, but the insects had already moved on for their next onslaught. Once they are in the soil, only flooding can destroy them although as they cannot live in sand, such vines as are grown on virtual sand dunes (such as those of Colares) are not troubled by them.

It was a Frenchman, Monsieur Planchon of Montpellier University, who named this insect *Phylloxera vastatrix*. Louis Pasteur had already confirmed that the louse originated from vines imported from North America. It could not have been indigenous to Europe, otherwise it would have wiped out the vine as a species and become extinct itself due to the lack of food.

The solution eventually adopted in north Portugal, as in all the other European wine regions, was to graft the European grape variety on to the resistant American root stock. This procedure is still carried out today, although nurseries of American stock are raised in each wine region and not imported each year from the U.S.A.

From 1868 to 1885 the Phylloxera louse systematically ravaged the Douro. Fortunately, 1868, 1870, 1872 and 1873 were all years when good quality port was produced in above-average abundance, before the dreaded louse had really got a hold. Many wine merchants in Great Britain had already taken steps to purchase forward stocks of port to be kept in Oporto so as to carry them through the projected famine years. The next four years, 1874–78, saw drastically reduced production and rising prices, coupled with inclement weather.

The Phylloxera was working its way down the River Douro and its tributaries, attacking the Cima Corgo first, taking away the quality wines. So what little port there was being produced was lacking in the better wines and having to rely on the lesser quality area of the Baixo Corgo.

Taking nine quintas at random, those of Lobata, Seixo, Trevões, Leyedinho, Cachucha, Pezinho, Ujo, Sopas and Oliveirinho, the total production in 1875 was 496 pipes. In 1879 it had fallen by about two-thirds, to 186 pipes. Various remedies were tried (like sulphust of carbon) in 1879 without much success. 1880 produced relative quantity and 1881 produced undoubted quality. However, as the quantity was so small, there was much foreboding in London's West End clubs, famous for their cellars and proud of their port, that vintage port was in danger of extinction. Dire thoughts, indeed!

Several temporary remedies using natural and artificial manures were used in 1882 and 1883. But by now the damage had really been done. The louse had already moved on and by August 1874 it had attacked the vineyards in southern Portugal. The Cima Corgo looked like a barren graveyard with just a few blackened dead vines to be seen on the terraces. But the turning point had come. The American root stocks, especially the *Vitis rupestris*, were now demonstrating their immunity to Phylloxera when grafted to the native grape variety.

Gradually life began to ebb back into the vineyards as relieved farmers and shippers alike realized that, given time, their livelihood need not be abandoned. It is difficult to conceive nowadays, with all our welfare state assistance, what it must have been like for a farmer in the Douro during this devastating period: no vines meant no wine – which meant no income. The dole had not been invented. He was on his own with little or no creature comforts, entering each winter with pathetic prospects at the other end. His land was unable, except in small patches, to be cultivated for anything except vines – it was too poor. Animals could not thrive in flocks, wild birds and game could only be occasionally caught. Even today, there are Douro farms of a fair size which are much as they would have been a century ago, with no electricity or running water. Farmers have an instinct for survival; they needed it then.

To begin with, the wines made from grafted stock were a bit lighter in colour and texture, and matured more quickly. Gradually, as the vines themselves became more mature, the wines became more robust and fruity. But, to those who can remember, they do not seem to have the long-lasting qualities of ungrafted stock – although as, these days, it is a costly business to have to keep wine for forty or fifty years before it is drinkable, this is not necessarily a bad thing.

Although Quinta da Roêda planted some ungrafted vines to mark Croft's tercentenary year, only Quinta do Noval has always kept a vineyard of ungrafted vines. These four thousand vines produce on average three pipes each year of "nacional" port. The dominant grape varieties are the Tourigas, Tinta Francisca and Roriz and the wine produced is full and hard, with a deep colour, and it lasts many, many years, as anyone who has ever tasted the Noval 1931 made from ungrafted vines will testify.

The wine region

The demarcated wine producing region in the Douro Valley covers 243,000 hectares. Only about 10 per cent, 24,000 hectares, are planted today with vines. The remaining land is either so rocky and mountainous that nothing can grow on it or crops such as olive trees, apples, and almonds are cultivated.

The whole area is divided into two basic parts – the Baixo, or lower, Corgo and the Cima, or upper, Corgo. This became necessary as it was clear that the wines produced from vines grown to the east of Regua did not have such benefit of the schistous rock as the vines that were planted between Regua and the Spanish frontier. The frontier is not only a political frontier but also a natural one and it does in fact represent a complete geographical change. The high plateau that extends eastwards from Mesão Frio ends at this juncture and falls away to plains. The Portuguese describe this plateau as "an island in granite" and it is essential to port's uniqueness. The vines east of Regua were usually more abundant in quantity and the wines not so fine in quality. The River Corgo thus became the dividing line. As a general guideline, even though the prices of grapes in each area are now roughly the same, the standard ruby and tawny brands come from the Baixo Corgo and the quality ports, old tawnies and vintage ports usually come from the Cima Corgo.

In most wine regions, it is possible to calculate how much wine is produced in so many hectares (one hectare=2.4 acres). In the Douro Valley it is impossible, as there are so many obstacles and other crops within any given hectare that it would become meaningless. Olive trees are the most widespread crop after the vines, as the olive resembles the vine in being able to grow where no other crop can thrive. Some decades it pays farmers to give over more land to olives if there is a depression in the sales of port; in other decades, such as the 1970s, olive trees were being uprooted by the thousand and furious vine planting was taking place. The Baixo Corgo on average yields three to four pipes of must or 3000 kg of must for every thousand vines; the Cima Corgo, because the schistous soil makes it harder for the vine to find water to swell the grapes, yields between one and two pipes of must, or 1125 kg, for every thousand vines.

The phrase always used by port shippers to describe their visiting their vineyards is "going up the Douro". Thus, going up the Douro from Oporto, one's first glimpse of terraced vineyards is just beyond Mesão Frio, a delightful elongated village full of solid white walls, green doors and children playing in the street obstructing traffic. The Baixo Corgo stretches on the south bank from Barró to Temilobos, and on the north bank from Barqueiros to Abaças, which is at the north of one of the Douro's larger tributaries, the River Corgo. Many people believe that the Cima Corgo then covers the whole area from this point to the Spanish frontier. In fact, the Cima Corgo proper only goes to the Cachão, and the area beyond what were the rapids is officially demarcated as Douro Superior. Small alterations to the area, according to what had shown to be convenient or advisable, were ratified in 1908. Further adjustments were made in 1921. Since then, the demarcated zone first outlined in 1756 has remained unaltered.

The landmass covered by vineyards in each of these areas is in Baixo Corgo 29 per cent, Cima Corgo 10 per cent and Douro Superior 3 per cent. The further towards Spain you go, the more difficult it is to plant vineyards, on account of the harshness of the terrain. Instead, typical small-farmer crops of wheat, cabbages and potatoes abound. Juxta-positioned, it is conceivable and indeed commonplace to see a single little vineyard that has probably been cultivated by several generations of the same family and its wines sold, on a handshake and without written agreement, to the same shipper year after year. This vineyard might be the size of Romanée Conti (2 hectares); it could produce the port that would go into an unsurpassable 30-year-old tawny or a 1927 or 1963 vintage. Yet it will be unmarked, merely terraced as are all the others, otherwise anonymous to the visitor, but just as lovingly cared for as any of its famous French counterparts.

Vineyard production

There are approximately 85,000 vineyards today, belonging to 28,000 farmers. The number of farmers is likely to increase rather than decrease, as Portuguese families adhere to the Napoleonic law which naturally dissects each family holding even further, because property cannot be willed away from the family and must be divided between all the successors when the owner dies. Of these 28,000 farmers, just under half, about 13,500, produce wine that is made into port; the remaining 14,500 farmers keep their wine as table wine. So half the vineyards seen in the Douro valley are producing table wine. It used to be that farmers were paid according to the degrees baumé or the sweetness of their grapes, and often table wine suppliers offered a higher rate than the port shippers to the respective farmers. Today, however, more formalized contracts between farmer and shipper are usually agreed.

Production

The breakdown of the production limits of these 13,500 farmers is:

70% produce less than	5,000 litres per annum
24% produce between	5,000–25,000 litres per annum
5% produce between	25,000–75,000 litres per annum
.6% produce between	75,000–150,000 litres per annum
.06% produce more than	150,000 litres per annum

This means that there are 9,500 farmers who produce less than 6,700 bottles of port per annum, and only 8 farmers or companies that produce more than 200,000 bottles each year. It is definitely an industry of individuals.

There are 170 million vines currently being cultivated in the Douro, of which 130 million are over twenty-five years old. As the maximum age in terms of economic usefulness of a vine is around 35 to 40 years, there is going to have to be a major replanting operation in the next ten years. Undoubtedly, the longer it is left the more expensive it will be.

Co-operatives

Over the past twenty-five years, the Portuguese government has gradually developed the co-operative system in all its wine producing regions. So now there are three kinds of producers; the shippers themselves, the co-operatives and the traditional farmers. Local farmers, who often do not have the economic means to buy modern equipment to produce the wine from their grapes, benefit the most from the co-operatives, and there is a clear tendency away from small producing units towards larger, more efficient wine centres. Farmers become partners in their nearest co-operative by taking the grapes at vintage time to these centres where they are given a credit card for the weight of grapes supplied. So far as the farmer is concerned, that is where his responsibility ends; he does not know or care whether his grapes become table wine or are fortified to become port.

Co-operatives in the Douro were originally designed to cater for the vinification of the surplus wine that was produced in excess of what the government decreed could be made into port. Thus, they were not allowed to make port, just good strong Douro wine. Recently, and not before time, there has been an upgrading of co-operatives, they have become accepted and are part of the established trading pattern. Co-operatives in major areas such as Regua, Moncorvo and Alijó have matured into wine centres in their own right. Provided that quality is upheld and proper control exercised, they are likely to play an increasingly important part in the port trade as a positive buffer between the smaller producers and the exporting shippers.

Government control

The Portuguese government, ever since the Marquês de Pombal got involved in the wine trade over two hundred years ago, has always kept the port trade firmly under its wing. Through various departments, the government controls port from the initial planting of vines, right through until it is bottled and exported – from the vine to the glass.

In 1933 the Salazar government decided to formalize the control that it was in fact already exercising. It appointed one main body – the Instituto do Vinho do Porto (the Port Wine Institute) and two others who were to be responsible to it, the Casa do Douro (the Farmers and Wine Growers Association) and the Gremio (since the Revolution in 1974 known as Associação) dos Exportadores do Vinho do Porto (the Port Wine Shippers' Association).

The Instituto do Vinho do Porto directs and controls the production and trading of port. Very little happens or can happen without the tentacles of the Instituto do Vinho do Porto's power being felt by those involved in the port trade. Its headquarters are in Oporto, just across the river from all the shippers' offices in Vila Nova de Gaia. The President of the Instituto do Vinho do Porto has the tightrope task of satisfying the grape farmers in the Douro, maintaining the overall quality of Portugal's most famous wine, encouraging and sometimes restraining both the British and the Portuguese port shippers in their export endeavours, and at the same time carrying out the policies and whim of whichever government is currently in power. Port is often quoted as being the most controlled of quality wines; it certainly is the only one which has its own entreposto or entrepôt which is still defined geographically by the spasmodic sentry boxes in Vila Nova de Gaia – these are now symbolically filled, but the power of the Instituto do Vinho do Porto is real enough in that its inspectors can enter any shipper's lodge and demand information if they are not happy with the conduct of any shipper.

The Instituto do Vinho do Porto has several main functions that constantly affect the port trade. In conjunction with the Casa do Douro it decrees how much wine produced in the Douro each year may be fortified into port, also the minimum and maximum prices that farmers and shippers must pay each other (this is communicated to the shippers just before each vintage and announced in the daily newspapers). It controls annual shipping rights, which are governed by the relation between the annual shipments of each shipper and their stocks held at the end of the fiscal year. In legal terms, this means that each shipper can only export in any given twelve months one-third of his stock held at the beginning of each year. This does mean that, in especially successful years, the shipper cannot export to meet orders at the end of the year if he has already exhausted his shipping rights that year. In theory it is a good law, as it is designed to ensure that the shippers mature their wines for a minimum of three years before they ship. In practice, this "Lei de Terço" can be quite unnecessarily restricting.

The Instituto do Vinho do Porto also monitors movement of all port within the entreposto and most importantly of all, tastes and analyses all blends in its increasingly up-to-date laboratories. It then issues each export shipment with a seal of guarantee (the "selo de garantia") and a certificate of origin, without which port is not port.

The Casa do Douro is the association to which all farmers must belong. Its headquarters are in Regua, the official capital of the port region and a town not noted for its cleanliness or great beauty. The Casa do Douro authorizes the plantation of new vineyards and the fortification of must. It is also responsible for checking that all vinification operations carried out during the production of port in the Douro are correct and satisfactory to all relevant parties. The Casa do Douro's prime role is that of government broker. It should buy and store wines in excess years and release wines during short years, thus keeping a constant flow available to port shippers. This important function needs clarifying by the government.

The third body, the AEVP, or the Port Shippers' Association, represents the port shippers. Whereas all port shippers, British and Portuguese, had to be members of its predecessor, the Gremio, not all shippers have to be members today of the AEVP. Its head-quarters are in Oporto, it meets regularly, and it does what all wine shippers' associations do. It is a vital forum for trade discussions, political improvements and sounding board for those who feel hard done by. The president has two other fellow directors, one Portuguese and one British, to assist him. The AEVP is responsible to the Instituto do Vinho do Porto for all matters concerning the blending, maturing and shipping of port in Vila Nova de Gaia.

Douro farmers and their work cycle

Man has never been able to change God's timing. Harvesting throughout the world takes place when the fruit is ripe. The grapes in the Douro Valley ripen to their optimum towards the end of September each year – sometimes, the vintage does not start until early October, but all grapes are usually picked and crushed by the third week in October.

In basic terms, little has changed over the past two hundred years in the making of port. The yearly cultivation cycle begins in November, with the same grape varieties, then there is the fortification of the must thereby producing port, the taking of the new wine to Oporto the following spring, followed by the maturing of different blends in separate vats until the port is shipped to the outside world. Indeed, the hardy peasants, with their unshaven faces, black hats and baggy trousers, toiling away in the terraced vineyards using much the same tools as their fathers and grandfathers before them, have not changed much either. Nor have the seemingly unending discussions regarding prices between farmer and shipper.

It is a western prerogative for the farmer to complain. He is always being hard done by. Some farming families, however, enjoy a marvellous relationship with shippers to whose predecessors they have sold their grapes for generations, even centuries; this is usually so in the better vineyards and with the more famous shippers. For example, the Carvalho family in the beautifully situated Ribalonga Valley in the Cima Corgo have been selling grapes to Croft for over 120 years. Croft can always rely on grapes from this region and it is pockets of vineyards such as this that, over the years, have helped formulate the basis of a "house style"; as no shipper owns more vineyards than can supply more than 5 per cent of his needs in terms of wine, each year he must buy in 95 per cent plus of the total amount of wine that he wants to make. A shipper's house style is most evident in vintage ports, so, when Croft declares a vintage, almost certainly some of the wine in it will have come from the Ribalonga Valley.

Other farmers believe that their grapes or wine are so especially good (Where has that been heard before . . . ?) that they must demand a higher price than that offered. It is then that ill-feeling has to be avoided by long and delicate negotiations between farmer and shipper. The latter presents the case of "We are already at the level of the price the market can stand"; the farmer pleads inflation and may even threaten to sell to another shipper unless he is paid more. All this takes place during three or four weeks at vintage time, which is busy enough anyway, but after several sleepless nights on both sides and protracted bargaining, hands are shaken and teeth are bared in smiles again, as each party basically understands that they need each other and realizes that they will have to talk again on the same lines in twelve months' time.

However, important and subtle changes have been taking place in the production of port in the last twenty years. In order to appreciate the whys and wherefores of these, the processes that take place in the Douro must be clearly understood.

Vines

Apart from marvelling at the human endeavour necessary to plant rows and rows and rows of vines on such inhospitable slopes in the middle of nowhere, the wine student will also marvel at the fact that there are no less than forty-eight different grape varieties used in the Douro Valley.

The principal one is the descendant of the Pinot Noir from Burgundy, originally brought to Portugal by Count Henry of Burgundy in about 1095 and further strengthened by newer cuttings also brought from Burgundy in the 17th century by a Scot named Robert Archibald who, having acquired Quinta de Roriz as a shooting lodge, wished to experiment with growing grapes there. This grape, now called the Tinta Francisca or Tinta Francesa, is the most popular grape used today for port.

It is strange to think that such a noble drink as port should have forty-eight varieties within it; if you think of Jerez you think of the dominant Palomino, of Bordeaux you think of both types of Cabernet, for fine Burgundy there is only the Pinot Noir. To understand why so many different varieties are necessary is to understand the complexities of the Douro Valley. The whole area covers some 900 square miles (2,000 sq. kms.), and the contrasting and unlikely soils are subject to very definite micro climates. This means that the temperature, rainfall and exposure to the sun of one quite small plot – the size of a town garden, say – will be really different from that of an adjoining section of vineyard, higher up, lower down, or slightly round the corner of a curve of hillside. No one grape variety could cope with nature's differences. That is why, in a vineyard covering fifty or one hundred hectares it has been quite common to see ten to fifteen different grape varieties.

In traditional vineyards, there has been a considerable regrafting of white varieties into red and hardly any of the new plantations have been grafted with white varieties due to price and market requirements. It is the red – or black – grapes that are the foundation of port. An estimate might be that the Douro now produces approximately 75 per cent red wine and 25 per cent white wine for port.

Although there are so many grape varieties and, in the past, vineyards often contained numerous different types, a certain amount of rationalisation has now taken place. It may be said that although single grape varieties do not make a good glass of port, it is not necessary to have ten to fifteen varieties in your glass; four or five well chosen ones will suffice.

Each is different; the balance of the finished wine is achieved by a judicious selection of the right weight of the different wines in the blend. The best varieties used most widely today are the Mourisco, Tinta Francisca, Tinta Amarela, Tinta Cão and Touriga Francesa. The Mourisco grapes are large, not very strong on colour, thin skinned but produce an excellent quality. The Tinta Francisca is probably the most popular, it is resistant to oïdium, one of the diseases of the wine vine, and produces round, violet tinted grapes, which are succulent and juicy. The Tinta Amarela is very dark with a light brown stem. The Tinto Cão produces a smaller grape and the Touriga Francesa always gives body to a blend, as it produces a stout, thick grape.

Interspersed between these top varieties are grapes of extremes: the Sousão has fantastic colour, the Malvasia Preta only grows in the limited area between Tua and Roncão and is very sweet, the Rufete is very aromatic, whilst the Tinta Carvalha is very thin skinned and rather insipid. The Bastardo is now rarely found, whereas the Roriz produces possibly the finest grade musts and highest sugar content of them all.

It is only recently that professional and technical experiments have taken place concerning the most economical and efficient way of planting aimed at maintaining, if not overall improving, the quality of the musts. The official state viticultural centre at Quinta Santa Barbara has 129 different hybrids, based on the above 48 basic varieties, under study at the time of writing. There is widespread agreement by the shippers and the more progressive farmers that more selective work needs to be done in this direction. The traditional hit or miss theory must be relied on less, more the professional computerized selective practice.

José Antonio Rosas of Ramos Pinto, a leading Douro expert, is a particularly articulate exponent of the need to increase quality and quantity from the vineyards: production per vine must increase, otherwise the costs of production per unit are going to be too high for comfort. Equally, the number of grape varieties "can be reduced down to three or four varieties" that, judiciously juxtaposed, will satisfy all the component parts needed in any given blend. It is only in the last few years – not surprising I suppose when you consider how conservative the farmers, shippers and port consumers are – that some major quintas have split up their new plantings into separate rows for different varieties. I believe this process will be accelerated in the next few years. The more progressive shippers are already exchanging information with other fortified wine producers in other countries, notably California, South Africa and Australia.

Traditionally, the root stock most popular in the region was the Montícula, which has now been replaced to a large extent in new plantations by R99, both strains being derived from the *rupestris* family.

Fertilizers

This is an aspect of vineyard work that visitors tend to overlook. But it is an essential part of the annual routine and, today, the effect of fertilizers on wine is an important matter.

Over-fertilization using too much nitrogen tends to increase production, repress colour formation and reduce sugar content. A happy medium must exist, however, between optimum quality and quantity, which is sufficient to keep the farmer in business. In former times some use was made of nitrogen fixing crops, such as lupins, which were sown and later ploughed into the vineyards; this type of fertilization provided a slow release of nutrients, coupled with a large percentage of organic matter which tended to make the soil more friable and increased its ability to retain moisture. However, some shippers used to say that the use of lupins affected the flavour of the wine.

There is still considerable controversy over the use of fertilizers, especially in new vineyards. It is certain, however, that, without their application, the vines would only survive with great difficulty and the production of grapes would be uneconomic.

A typical fertilization programme for a new plantation would be as follows:

On ploughing and cutting terraces, a long-lasting slow leaching fertilizer is applied, giving potassium, nitrogen, and phosphorus, possibly with trace elements. This is very useful when the roots of young vines are established, causing a spurt in growth in three-year-old vines, sooner or later, according to its depth of application. For the root stock, application of urea is often made in the first year, which gives an immediate release of nitrogen and consequent increase in vegetative growth. After grafting, both chemical and organic fertilizers are normally applied until the vines are established, after which fertilizers are normally applied in alternate years to maintain the vines in a healthy condition. Modern foliage fertilizers are now applied in some vineyards, mixed with the fungicidal sprays.

Unfortunately, the modern chemical and organic fertilizers do very little to modify the physical nature of the soil or to increase its ability to retain moisture. Traditional fertilization with lupins or humus, as already described, is almost impossible to do nowadays because of difficulties in obtaining labour. However, recently, some interest has been shown in using treated town garbage which provides both volume of organic material and a slow leaching of nutrients.

There is still very much to be learnt both about fertilization and vine spacing, in terms of optimum quality-quantity ratios.

Terracing

For centuries terraced vineyards have been the undisputed hallmark and attraction of the Douro Valley. These beautifully built dry-stone walls permitted the maximum rows of vines, sometimes of up to ten, though more usually of two to four rows, to be cultivated on a flat surface. Consider – 90 per cent of the demarcated port area has gradients of over 30 per cent and vines can be found on slopes with 40 to 70 per cent gradients – the sight provides breathtaking views, bewilderment at the time taken, a majestic panorama that seems to go on and on and is unlike that of any other wine region. Like other crops grown through time past in this mountainous region, vines were grown on terraces; the main reason was to prevent soil erosion and stop them being washed away by heavy winter rains pouring down the slopes to the river. The corollary was that, during the winter months, the rain would lie deep down on the schistous rock, so that the roots of the vine could secure themselves by digging two metres down into earth and thereby could drink during the hot rainless summer weeks.

Time was no object in those bygone days, nor was labour. Villages and villagers alike depended on wine for their livelihood, whole families worked in the vineyards all through the year. Terracing was just something that had to be done, and it was done beautifully, too. These people seldom ventured away from their farms, except occasionally to Regua, or perhaps to Oporto for a special occasion. Then, suddenly, the way of life changed. The first television set appeared in the Douro. Live communication bred unrest. Sons began to look at their fathers and grandfathers with ideas not so much of treading in their footsteps, but, like Dick Whittington, of going out and making their fortunes. Young and not so young but able men left in droves the Douro Valley which had housed them for so long, to find industrial work which gave them a new outlook on life and embryonic independence – as it paid better. Some stayed in Oporto, some journeyed south to Lisbon, but the more adventurous went to France, either to stay or as a starting point to the rest of Europe. Others were conscripted to fight in the various African wars; they sent money back to their families, which now consisted of old folk, grass widows and young children and, on occasional visits back home, they often built houses and thereby injected cash into the Douro.

But this was no substitute for an honest pair of working hands. The vineyards show the result of this trend to leave the Valley. Few terraces have been built since it started. It would not be so bad if former generations had not in many cases built such narrow terraces that only one row of vines can be grown there; mechanisation on this basis is impractical. Even the smallest tractor cannot work in this space.

Much thought is going into this problem. In the mid-sixties, bulldozers began to have quite an effect on the Douro scenery. Two new types of terracing, which directly affect modern planting methods, are being introduced for the future: horizontal and inclined terracing. As in most spheres of life, the pendulum of change can swing too quickly in the opposite direction; if terraces could not be built by man, then they must go. So, recently, the hills of the Douro have been active with 180 horsepower bulldozers, heaving and weaving great boulders of schist in an attempt to level vineyards as much as possible by creating wider steps for the vines to grow on. Inclined terracing, efficient though not so beautiful as the former hand-made type, has one main disadvantage; as many rows of vines are planted on the widened terrace, it is difficult to use automated machinery there because there is not enough space.

The bulldozed horizontal terrace is probably going to be more in demand in the future, because, although 40 per cent of potential vineyard space is lost, with only two rows of vines in each terrace, these rows are planted far enough apart (moving away from the traditional 1.00m/1.30m to 2.50m of space between rows) to accommodate automated machinery. Tractors which straddle vines are also used in many flat areas with great success; they can be used for spraying, digging between the vines, and some day surely they will become sufficiently advanced mechanically to pick and even prune as well.

Three main difficulties prevent the expansion necessary to produce sufficient wines to meet demand. First the geographical barriers to mechanization; second, lack of government investment grants; third, there is no planting legislation.

Classification of the vineyards

Maintaining quality at the same time as keeping to a vineyard classification (as in the Médoc in 1855) over such diverse terrain as the Douro proved quite a task for the Casa do Douro when it was set up in 1933. After careful study, the points system was adopted, which in essence meant that a maximum of 1680 points was awarded to each vineyard, based on production, soil, gradient, altitude, geographical position, position in relation to climatic conditions, upkeep and maintenance, qualities of grapes and age of vines. Each vineyard was then graded according to the number of points the inspectors awarded it. Decreasing grades meant that correspondingly less wine produced per 1000 vines could be made into port. This system has stood the test of time and although it is rare for a vineyard to go up or down a grade, the scheme is respected and works well. The classic vineyard slopes gently on schistous rock, and faces south-east at an altitude of 200 to 300 metres above sea level, although planting in the flatter areas is likely to be a key development in future years.

The average rainfall in the Douro ranges from 90 cm at Regua, down to 40 cm at Barca d'Alva on the Spanish frontier. Experiments in irrigation, especially in the use of underground systems, are being carried out to capitalize on all the rainfall. The temperature dives below zero in the winter and burns to 45 degrees in the summer.

The year in the vineyard

The work in the vineyards, leading up to the climax of the vintage, really starts at the end of October or beginning of November. The colouring of the vineyards then is wonderful; the lights of dawn, midday, late afternoon and dusk play unbelievable, sensual themes on the vivid autumnal vines. Striking hues of red, yellow and purple, set against the backcloth of rounded mountain ranges, welcome the workers back to the vineyards after the excitement of the vintage weeks.

Pruning

November sees the start of pruning. Both old and new plantations use a Guyot type of head pruning, which consists of leaving a fruiting cane and a spur, the spur producing fruit in the following season. Several of the more modern plantations are using the bilateral cordon, which has been recommended by the government authorities both to increase production and to make mechanization easier. The bilateral cordon is used in Portugal in areas of high production, on more fertile soils. Whether or not it proves successful in the Douro is yet to be seen; as yet, there is some doubt.

Once a vineyard is established, the amount of pruning done to any one vine is naturally a function of the vine's strength; weaker vines are pruned to bear less fruit until they become stronger with age.

At the same time as this specialist task takes place, the unskilled workers start digging trenches around the vines in order to catch and divert as much rain water as possible to the roots. The winter months can be cruel on the hillside; this is reflected in the ruthless pruning method, which only leaves one shoot on each side of the vine.

Soil preparation

February and March are the months for preparing the soil for new American rootstocks in new vineyards. Fertilizers, many organic, are applied. Vineyards are now mostly deep ploughed so the one-year-old American root stock is planted in holes 50cm deep. Grafting also takes place at this time; the soil is removed from the base of each vine. The American vine, now cut back, is split with a knife, the national grape variety is inserted, bound with raffia and then covered up.

Flowering and grape formation

April sees the first green shoots appear and the first spraying against oïdium with Bordeaux mixture takes place in May. Tiny yet precise flowers give way to equally tiny yet precise bunches of grapes. June 24th, St John's Day, can witness the first tracing of colour on the grape skins, this development being described as O Pintor, the painter, arriving in the Douro. "The painter has been round," say those who have noted the way the grapes begin to turn from their early pale green.

July, August and September are the months which determine the quality and quantity of each vintage. Frequent spraying, guarding, weed-killing, leaf removing and care are exercised by the farmers during this period. At least one eye however is always kept upwards

to the sky; sun to ripen and rain to swell the grapes are indications of
success – too much or too little of either at the wrong time can ruin in
a few days what man has worked at the whole year.

The vintage

Vintage time in any wine region is a time for rejoicing. It is the
culmination of the year's work, the results are the yardstick by which
a farmer, his family, an entire village or a company are held in esteem
by their peers. It also has a magical sound about it. Mention vintage
to a wine lover and invariably a smile, reminiscent or anticipatory,
is evoked.

The vintage in the Douro is an amazing happening, though less so
now that economic factors are gradually, but, it must be admitted,
not before time, replacing tradition. Still, the excitement is there –
the inevitable blend of tradition and the unknown. There is a feeling
of taking part in a really rather grand picnic. During the year the
shippers still base themselves in Oporto, although someone in the
company will forage in the Douro every ten days or so, but at vintage
time they transport themselves lock, stock and barrel to their quintas
for a whole month.

The average date over the years when picking starts is September
20th and throughout the region it takes three to four weeks. Each
shipper decides when to start: he is in constant communication with
all the farmers from whom he is going to buy and discusses with them
when they should mobilize the band of pickers. The microclimates
invariably mean that some vineyards are more advanced than others;
these will be picked first. It is an almost military operation, carried
out by motley bands of villagers whose families have been on call for
this annual ritual for centuries.

The weather is hot; the wine is plentiful. That much has not
changed. But many changes have taken place in the past twenty or so
years. Until about 1960, there was plenty of labour and a respected
master/servant relationship existed between shippers and farmers.
Here are accounts of what used to happen – and what did happen
until very recently – and what occurs up the Douro now.

A traditional vintage

In addition to making wine at his own quinta or vineyard, the shipper would probably buy from as many as fifty to a hundred farmers. On an appointed day, he would visit each one, inspect the tonels or vats in the farmer's winery in which the newly made wine would be stored, and be proffered a glass of delicious Douro old tawny port that had never left the farmer's sight. Idle gossip and time-honoured bantering about the farmer's wife would conceal the gentle haggling about the price for which the wine would be sold and eventually a handshake and enough indiscreet comment to make the wife blush would seal the deal.

Merry bands of pickers would then descend on the quinta. These bands are called *rogas* and their leader is the *rogador*. At the end of the vintage, they would present a symbolic harvest offering, usually a flowered garland on a pole, to the lady of the house, although at least one port house never permitted women – apart from the workers – to go to their quinta at vintage time. The accordion is as much part of their equipment as are the sharp knives for cutting and the wooden baskets (weighing 60 kilos) for carrying the grapes. They pick to music, carry to music, eat to music, dance to music in the evening and probably dream to music at the end of their exhausting days. The vintagers used to transport the baskets either on their shoulders for short distances or by bullock cart for longer distances – hot, sweaty work, but it had to be done.

At the winery, the grapes were then tipped into a *lagar*, a granite walled square trough, usually thirty feet long and four feet high, of a sufficient capacity for twenty or thirty pipes of wine to be made from it.

While the women were out picking (to music), the men used to leap, often fourteen at a time linking arms, into the lagar and start treading (to music). Always dressed in blue, with their trousers pulled right up, they trod, barefoot, four hours on and four hours off, marching back and forth in a line in the lagar, or breaking rank from time to time, until the grapes were crushed and the juice floating on top of the mass of pulpy residue. To cut the lagar is an extremely hard job – the biblical comment of one who "has trodden the winepress all alone" shows that it has always been so, and the encouragement of the music, wine, a cigarette and the jocular comments of fellow workers is not just fun.

Something that other books do not relate is that small holes in the outer walls of the lagar were drilled at the right height and suitably distanced so that a wine-filled treader could relieve himself without suffering the indignity of leaving his work and leaping out of the lagar. I have never actually witnessed usage of this escape valve, nor have I seen workers wash their feet before they started treading (although squeamish visitors are always told that they do), but I have seen them wash them afterwards – although the must dyes the skin purple.

The must starts fermenting, becoming darker the whole time as the colour is drawn from the skins. Boards are then placed across the lagar for the men to stand on and stir the must with *maçacos* (paddles) to keep the fermentation going. When the sugar content has converted enough of itself to alcohol, according to the judgment of the wine maker, the newly made wine is run off into the wooden vats at the same time as the *aguardente* (grape brandy at 77 per cent by volume) is added at a ratio of 440 litres of wine to 110 litres of aguardente. This arrests the fermentation and the wine, now in wooden "*tonels*" or barrels, then officially becomes port.

If the wine were allowed to ferment right out with no residual sugar content, the result would be a harsh dry red wine if made only with red grapes – not very appetising. Red port must therefore also contain an element of sweetness to make it acceptable to the palate.

On the other hand, white port, which is made in exactly the same way as red port but only with white grapes, can be fermented out to a much further degree – even so that all the sugar is converted into alcohol; a dry white port is one of each shipper's specialities (see pp. 55, 57).

The wine, or rather port, then used to stay in the tonels, being regularly tasted and in the spring following the vintage was transported down the River Douro in *barcos rabelos*. These were magnificently sturdy sailing boats, fashioned after the Viking boats which first made their appearance in Portugal over a thousand years ago. Flat-bottomed, with a square sail and elongated rudder, these traditional Douro boats used to take aboard up to sixty pipes of port down the Douro on each journey. It took three days and three nights to reach Oporto; each boat was fully stocked with *bacalhau* (codfish), roast *cabritos* (kid), suckling pigs, oranges and, of course, bread. The crew of four slept on board. The swirling waters and dangerous rapids must have made each journey an epic race against nature. George Robertson in *Port* describes how he, with Robin Reid, both from Croft, John Smithes and Felix Vigne from Cockburn joined forces with their wives to emulate such a journey in 1953, and for three days they virtually dropped out of the twentieth century – a great experience.

A modern vintage

Now that the Douro Valley, the underdeveloped north-west region of Portugal, has fewer able-bodied workers, major changes have been and still are taking place. True, the *rogas* still tramp forth from their villages at vintage time and the women pick the grapes – but they have been known to strike. Music is still important and at many of the quintas, the men still sleep in one dormitory and the women in another. The wine is arrested with aguardente and the ensuing port is taken to Vila Nova de Gaia next spring.

The main differences are the vinification process, the blending policies and the maturing and transport to the lodges in Vila Nova de Gaia.

The human foot process of crushing the grapes only really gave way to autovinification in the early 1960s, with the introduction of electricity on a general basis. Human feet could operate in the smallest quinta. Neighbouring farmers brought their grapes to their friends. The grapes were crushed, wine was made and port sold as per the handshake to the shipper. Mechanical crushing devices such as those installed in other wine regions proved unsatisfactory when used for port and until quite recently many people thought that nothing could improve on the human foot for the pressing. Gradually, however, with the introduction of autovinification, wine centres began to be established at the larger quintas. Sandeman and Croft were among the first. This tendency meant that the shipper wanted to buy more and more in grape form from the farmers and less in the form of wine. It suited both sides: the shipper was able to exercise more quality control on the actual wine making process – the farmer had not got the necessary labour anyway and was relieved of the keeping. Soon, the majority of wine was being made either by the French designed closed autovinification plants, or by open-tank fermentation.

To extract optimum colour or strength from the must, there is a strong school of thought that this can best be done now by using the open-tank fermentation method with automatic paddles which activate the must. This method judiciously combines the traditional with the modern. Lagars were knocked down though fortunately a few enterprising quintas have kept one or two for posterity. Technicians in white coats and talking foreign languages came to the quintas – the twentieth century had really arrived in the Douro.

The grapes now arrive in open rectangular steel containers perched on lorries. They are weighed before being tipped into a V-shaped reception tank, and are immediately fed by an electrically driven screw feeder into the crushing and stemming machine, which is an upright cylinder about one metre in diameter, which can remove a variable percentage of the stalks. Inside this cylinder, all or some of the stalks, depending on the tannin required, are extracted by centrifugal force. Stalks are mostly kept in if it is a hot year; in a green or wet year, the tannic content will be too high to achieve a balanced wine, so up to two-thirds of them will be discarded.

At the same time as the grapes are starting their initiation into becoming wine, a sample of the grape juice is taken and fed into a refractometer, an optical instrument used to measure the refractive index of a liquid. Using conversion tables, the refractive index can be converted into density readings, for measuring the sweetness or the potential alcohol content of grape musts. The refractometer has replaced the hydrometer in most modern wineries. The farmer is then paid according to the weight of his grapes and usually a bonus is given if the sugar content is higher than average.

The resultant must is then pumped through a network of pipes directly into the square concrete or triangular stainless steel tanks, usually referred to as autovinification vats. These vats are then filled up to 40cm from the top, the autovinificator cylinder is clamped down, the water escape valve is filled, and, provided that there are normal temperature conditions at around 16°C, the must will start to ferment naturally almost immediately and continues without anyone touching it, although careful supervision is maintained throughout.

The sugar content is continually checked during the two to three days of fermentation and, when the required degree is reached, according to the wine maker's judgment as well as his instruments, the must is drawn off into similar sized vats, where aguardente is added to arrest the fermentation. It is after this conjoining that the must becomes port wine.

Moving the wine

The young port wine still stays in wooden vats or cement holding tanks in the Douro until it is taken down to Vila Nova de Gaia in the spring. Tasting during this embryonic period is still done as it has been for generations by using a *tomboladeira*; this tasting cup is unique to the port trade and it may be made of either porcelain or silver. It is larger than the French tastevins, has a dome in the middle and a side like the lip of a dog's bowl, so that it can be held firmly in the hand. When the wine is agitated by a rhythmic hand movement, the colour and bouquet can be assessed. White porcelain tends to exaggerate the deep purple colour, whereas silver has the reverse effect. Tasting a very young, well-balanced port from this vessel is like tasting liquid velvet.

An easy formula to remember is "The earlier the fermentation is arrested, the sweeter the port". Micro-organisms cannot do their work of fermenting when the wine's alcoholic strength is above about 16 per cent alcohol by volume, because the alcohol kills off the yeasts. Any sugar remaining when fermentation stops or is stopped is left in the wine. If the original grape sugar content, measured in terms of Baumé, is 14 per cent and the fermenting must is drawn off when its sugar content has been reduced only to 6 per cent, 8 per cent of the total sugar will still be left. It is important to appreciate that the subtle underlying sweetness of port is the sweetness of the original sugar content of the grapes and nothing else.

White port

White port is made in the same way as red port, but only white grapes are used. However, as the skins of these grapes acquire a golden-brown hue at vintage time, it is necessary to minimize the contact with the skins during fermentation, in order to produce a light gold rather than a yellowy-white port, which would result from the pigments in the skins tinting the must. The skins are therefore removed from the must after the grapes have been crushed and the juice released.

The Douro "bake"

There is less rain and more sun in the Douro compared to the lodges
in Vila Nova de Gaia; consequently, port matured up country in the
Douro, as happens with some of the farmers' wines and some that
the shippers keep at their quintas, achieves a different nose and taste.
This is traditionally referred to as the Douro "bake" or "burn". To
my mind this is as sensational as it is uncommon to experience –
never miss the chance to try this rare style of port if you are offered a
glass while in the region. It conjures up to me the baking hot August
days of silence, broken perhaps only by the barking of a distant dog,
evoking all the intensities of the region, and demonstrating the skill
of the blender perfecting his art.

Maturing port

Now that technology is happily blending with skills handed down
from taster to taster, much study is being undertaken as to the ageing
and maturing of port. Port has always been stored in lodges in Vila
Nova de Gaia, partly because that was where the main operation
originally was, partly because young ruby wines left to mature in the
Douro extremes of climate would lose their firm vigour and
freshness, and partly because the climatic and living conditions in the
Douro in former times were not very pleasant on a 365-day basis.

Recently I enjoyed a tasting with Gordon Guimarãens of Cockburn's. In the tasting room in Vila Nova de Gaia we tasted two
samples of identical three-year-old ports; one had been matured in
the Douro and the other in Vila Nova de Gaia. There was a
pronounced difference in nose, colour and taste: the former – the
Douro-matured wine – was definitely rounder and had aged quicker.
So, unless one can guarantee proper temperature control of any
maturation cellar in the Douro, the obvious answer is to mature
older tawny ports in the Douro and younger ruby ports in Vila Nova
de Gaia. However, lack of space in Vila Nova de Gaia, already
crowded on the surface as is evident to the view, and government
pressure to develop the Douro region more, so as to revitalize the

countryside, may well lead those involved to mature more port in the Douro than hitherto. All these changes mean continuous structural improvements at the ever-developing wine co-operatives or the larger wine centres. Indeed Fernando van Zeller, of Noval, describes traditional quintas and wine centres beautifully and poetically as "unfinished symphonies"; it is to be hoped that they can be adapted to present demands and be "finished" by the assistance of modern improvements.

The great dams

In the early 1970s, in order to produce hydro-electric power in the Douro valley, a series of dams on the River Douro in both Spain and Portugal were begun. In 1974 the first one was completed just east of Regua; a gargantuan undertaking and a gargantuan change. Sandy beaches, rapids, granite ridges disappeared overnight, the river rose ten metres, a few vines were lost, but soon were replanted higher up. It had been thought that the difference to the river's level might affect the vineyards because the reflection from the water is of importance for its effect on the vines on the bank. This does not seem to be so even though the parched riverbeds of summer have now given way to a year round constant water surface. The result is a gorgeous twenty-mile lake, right in the middle of the best Douro vineyards – fishing and water ski-ing are a far cry from the old fashioned *barcos rabelos*. The Douro is not navigable yet, and judging from the water level below some dams – there are to be five in all – it will be some time until river transport can be used again.

The railways first took the trade away from the *barcos rabelos* in the 1930s, but trains had priced themselves out of the market by the 1960s so, since then, road tankers have been used to bring port down to Gaia. The winding roads still make the journey one of three hours, as for the railway journey.

Changes in blends selection

The other change that has recently taken place is that, whereas right up until the end of the 1960s, each shipper might have bought and tasted four hundred different blends of port, he now can assimilate these into, say, a hundred blends, from which he will supply his ten brands. For until around 1960, each wine merchant, each brewer, each university college and each major club wanted its own individual blend of port; samples of what was required were sent out to Portugal and these then had to be matched exactly, both in quality and in price. If one shipper could not fulfil these requirements, the sample was handed around to one who could. This was really a thoroughly unhealthy platform for planning and future brand development and, in addition to being somewhat of a "hit or miss" operation, it wasted a great deal of time for all concerned. As the port shippers reasserted themselves in the early 1970s, this way of working gradually ceased and, with it, the need to have so many individual *lotas* or blends on the market.

O RIO DOURO   THE RIVER DOURO
Huma Legoa acima do Salto   One League above the Salto
da Sardinha.   N.º 1.   da Sardinha.

IV
Port Maturation
in Vila Nova de Gaia

JUST AS IN September and October of each year the roads in the Douro Valley are crammed with shaky lorries transporting containers of grapes from vineyards to wine centres, so in every February and March, the roads in Vila Nova de Gaia are filled with sleek tanker lorries clambering over the cobbled maze, bringing the new wine into each shipper's lodge.

Because of the varied terrain, the ubiquitous micro-climates and the 28,000 farmers who produce the wine, the young ports that emerge after vintage time have many and different characteristics. This is why the port taster and blender is such a respected member of his company; he has to use his skills constantly over the next six months to taste, select and appraise each *lota* (blend). Each company has its own method and traditional yardsticks, but the principle is the same.

According to John Burnett the port trade's first Ph.D in bio-chemistry, apart from the essential technical knowledge, "tasters or those wishing to embark on this career should have the following characteristics: health and vigour, a good eyesight, an excellent memory and, above all, should be drinkers of port in their leisure hours, not just daily tasters!"

Before wine centres and cooperatives became established in the late 1960s and early 1970s, many more individual wines were made in each quinta's lagars. Now, over 80 per cent of all port made is produced in wineries. They are here to stay, as elsewhere in the wine world. Modern fermentation tanks and storage tanks are considerably larger than the average *lagar, tonel* and *balseiro* (vat) in the farmer's lodge. It is, therefore, impractical to keep as many individual *lotas* as before.

Cooperatives now account for about 40 per cent of all port produced. They are still in an embryonic stage concerning quality and have much to learn from the traditional port companies. Cooperatives must learn and the port companies must teach and then demand that sufficient attention is paid to quality. Although the average quality of the wine has improved over the past few years, there are still too few qualified technical staff.

Ports should be initially separated on more definitive characteristics than just sweetness. So long as the government regulates the maximum quantity to be made each year and stipulates minimum and maximum prices to be paid to the farmers, competition to buy the better quality grapes will continue. Instead of cooperatives and port companies turning their backs on each other, hoping the other will go away, it is in the interests of the maintenance of quality of port that technical aid and harmonious relationship be established between the two as much as possible.

This change from individual quinta production to modern winery techniques has been possible and welcomed, as during this time, concepts and methods of exporting port have also been changing. By and large, the port companies have joined the international wine and spirit jet set and have developed international brands to sell in major port markets. Instead of having over thirty different styles on their price lists, each with its own mark, such as ◇◇◇or ⌄◇⌄ which were used by different breweries for their pubs, the same shipper will nowadays present five or six different brands which would be recognizable in all markets. Port tasters, therefore, have fewer *lotas* to deal with.

Tasting is not quite such a full-time job as it used to be. More time is often taken up complying with the endless regulations and paperwork to satisfy each country's requirements. (Some countries' stipulations give the impression that a glass of well defined chemicals is required, rather than a beverage which gives health and happiness.)

The first tasting of the young, nubile port takes place in the Douro in November. This is the time to search out and isolate the wines' many and different characteristics. Different grape varieties from different micro-climates picked on different days will give different base wines. Excessive rain causes light wines; excessive sun gives concentration of fruit. Some will be big and fat, some will have too much tannin, others will be delicate and flowery. This first assessment can only give the taster an impression of the quality of the vintage; at the same time, he can immediately separate and treat any wines that are doubtful either as to their present condition or the potential contribution they may make to the finished wine. This tasting session is not held in a beautifully temperature-controlled tasting room or even in a cellar. Stamina is needed at this stage; tastings can last for six or seven hours, the taster standing in the windy doorway of a Douro lodge, swirling cold, young, often indigestible wines across the palate, with dogs wailing outside and usually rain cascading. Think of this first tasting when you next recline elegantly in a comfortable armchair enjoying a glass of port.

After this initial tasting, the wines are racked bright by being pumped off their lees into fresh casks as the wintery conditions help to precipitate some of the colouring matter, yeast and potassium salts of tartaric acid and these are left behind in the debris. The very young ports then "close up" sufficiently to be transported to Vila Nova de Gaia, ready for their first classification in early spring.

This second tasting, in which wines will be classified and first *lotas* are made up, is the most important. The basic idea is to decide on each wine's career by joining similar wines together and to separate the top quality wines, in case this year's wines are worthy of being declared a vintage; such wines have great depth, vigour, full colour and are well-balanced. These "crême de la crême" wines are then kept separate for two winters and a summer during these early formative years. If they then pass the test of the taster's reappraisal, they will become vintage port; if not, there will be no vintage port that year and these wines, still definitely in the top-quality range, will be blended in with other quality ports destined to become old tawny ports.

One leading taster in Vila Nova de Gaia says he recognizes quality wines at this stage by their delightful "cold tea" aroma. This stayed with the 1977s for a considerable time. By the year 2000 this initial aroma could easily blossom into one of the most attractive bouquets of any vintage port produced this century.

The third step after this classification is the blending process, which now starts always with a view in mind of the final type and style of wine required.

Unlike young sherry, which is always put into new butts, young port is always put into well seasoned vats or pipes. Wood ports, that is all ports that are not vintage ports, are always built on their forefathers in that there is a constant blending and dovetailing of wines together to ensure continuity; the new blend should always have a percentage of the previous wine in it. The concept is somewhat similar in practice to the solera system used in Jerez; red wines, especially red wines produced in such differing weather conditions as in the Douro, need more individual care and attention.

At this stage six-month old baby ports should have a clean flowery nose and their colour should be deep red, with a hint of blueish purple. A brownish tinge at the rim of the glass where the wine meets it indicates that the wine has been poorly made with overripe or rotten grapes; it is interesting that poorer quality wines assume a brownish colour much more rapidly than those of good quality – the maturation rate appears to be inversely proportional to the quality. On the palate the wine should be firm and give an impression of sweetness and body, the aftertaste should be clean, without any sense of cloying.

Young ports

The main channels that these young ports can now be fed into are as follows:

Style	Description	Approximate age
	RED	
A. Ruby	The natural and popular style of young port. Full-bodied, round and fruity.	3 years
Vintage character (non-vintage) or Late bottled vintage (with a date)	These fuller bodied ports are left to mature in wood longer. Firm, with depth, they have vintage connotations and characteristics.	4–6 years

Style	Description	Approximate age
	RED	
B. Tawny	Basic ruby port blended with white port. Often drier than ruby ports. Popular where port is consumed as an aperitif.	3–5 years
Old tawny or Dated ports or Ports with indication of age	After five years or so, colour of red port becomes naturally brown or tawny. Flavour becomes more concentrated, so old tawnies need refreshing with younger wines. Delightful well-balanced mature blends.	5–10 years (20-, 30- and 40-year-old ports available in limited quantities.
	WHITE	
C. White	Medium to sweet grapey taste. Ideal as full-bodied white aperitif.	3 years
Dry White	The port-shipper's natural aperitif. All companies have their own individual preferences, ranging from medium to bone dry. Light and gently nutty.	3–5 years

Red ports are aged in wooden vats and pipes. Pipes, stacked only four high to avoid undue evaporation, are the traditional maturing vehicles. White port gains colour if matured too long in wood, so cement or concrete vats are now most used for the maturation and storage of white ports. Blending, for both red and white ports, usually takes place in either concrete or large wood vats, although it used to be done in individual pipes. So the dictum is "Age in wood, blend in concrete".

If everything in the production process has gone right so far, all the port shipper and his port have to do now is to wait until the moment has come to draw off the wine, bottle it and sell it. For the port, that does not pose too many problems; slumbering away in a pipe, it has an easy life. The port shipper, however, is continually striving for better results.

The Douro Valley is producing lighter wines than it used to because of modern vinification methods and grafted vines; labour costs are constantly rising and so larger vats with a capacity varying from five pipes to four hundred pipes are being used more and more for aging wines. The rate of maturation depends on their size. The larger the volume, the slower the rate. As a consequence, wines are selected at an earlier age according to the style required and then stored in the appropriate-sized container. National and imported oak, chestnut and Brazilian mahogany are all used in Vila Nova de Gaia.

All wooden containers are extremely well-seasoned before use, using table wine and/or young red port. Therefore, very little woodiness is detectable in the wine, except possibly in the very oldest of tawnies matured in the Douro. Frequent racking to remove lees and to aerate the wine increases maturation and the choice of storage, either in the Douro or in Vila Nova de Gaia, together with the frequency of racking, profoundly affects the style of the finished wine.

In a traditional Douro lodge, seasonal temperature changes of up to 20°C in the wine, coupled with the fact that the atmosphere is very dry in comparison to Vila Nova de Gaia, leads to a much faster evaporation and maturation rate together with a rather baked or madeirized style. Relative humidity in Vila Nova de Gaia rarely drops below 54 per cent; therefore evaporation is lower and the temperature fluctuations under normal storage conditions rarely exceed 14–16°C, giving rise to a much slower maturation and a different, rather fresher, style to those wines matured in the Douro.

Owing to the limited storage capacity in Vila Nova de Gaia, the majority of companies are now keeping larger stocks in the Douro either in wood, to take advantage of the faster maturation rates, or in large cement tanks, as a temporary measure before wine is moved into wood in Vila Nova de Gaia.

Over the last decade, enormous advances have been made in the understanding of the complicated chemical reactions involved in the maturation of red wines; as a consequence, the maturation of wine can be controlled, which will involve the choice of container to be used and the number of rackings it should receive during its life. Wood storage of port is a method of controlled oxidation and the maturation of wine is mainly due to evaporation and the effects of oxygen.

When a particular blend is called forward by the taster to include it in a shipment of port that is about to be exported, certain processes are now used regularly to ensure that the wine remains bright and stable in the retail shop and in the customer's house. A cloudy wine always looks so unappetizing.

The traditional method of clarifying red wines is by fining. This process removes a certain amount of colour and tannin, which tends to make the wine softer and give it more age. Port is invariably filtered. Modern filters have now replaced the old-fashioned cloth bag method of separating the liquid from the lees, which can represent up to 6 per cent of the volume in the first racking. Modern filters use a series of woven nylon pads. Lees are circulated until there is an even coating of solid material on these pads. Once this is obtained, the solid cake acts as a filter medium and bright wine is obtained.

For white wines, bentonite, a naturally occurring clay, like earth, containing montmorillonite derived from volcanic ash, is used as a fining agent to remove proteins.

Most of the larger companies now stabilize their wines by refrigeration. The increased demand for bottling at source has led to more and more companies installing refrigeration equipment. It is estimated that 85 per cent of exports are now refrigerated. Now that the port shipper is directly responsible, as opposed to his traditional agent who used to do the bottling for him, the laboratory and technical staff play a much greater part in each company's payroll.

Chilling a wine down to within 2° of its freezing point results in the precipitation of both unstable colouring matter and the potassium salts of tartaric acid. Once chilled, the wine is either passed through a vessel to encourage the deposition of potassium hydrogen tartrate and then filtered (continuous refrigeration) or kept in an insulated tank for up to one week before filtering (Gasquet type process).

After cold filtering in both systems, the refrigerated wine is passed through a plate heat exchanger. In this plate exchanger the cold wine passes over thin stainless steel plates with wine at ambient temperature about to enter the refrigeration plant on the other side. Hence the new wine is partially chilled before entering the scraped surface heat exchanger and the cold refrigerated wine is warmed up.

Refrigeration and the addition of anti-oxidant sulphur dioxide before bottling means that it is possible to guarantee that the wine remains bright in bottle for eighteen months at least if kept under normal storage conditions. Some companies also briefly pasteurize their wines after this cold treatment. This is a technique used to heat liquids rapidly to heat-stabilize them against possible growth of micro-organisms or to remove compounds which are unstable at high temperatures. The flash type, which raises the wine to a very high temperature in a matter of seconds and then holds the wine at that temperature again for a brief period, is the best to use.

For final filtration, after fining or refrigeration, a Kieselguhr filtration followed by pad filtration is normally employed. Plate and frame filters with filter pads of various pore size are used to achieve final brilliance.

The port, having run this gauntlet of modern technology, is then ready to be bottled, stowed into cartons and exported. Bottling plants have improved enormously over the last ten years. As late as 1971, bottles were being delivered to bottling halls in large baskets, sitting heavily astride women's heads; now they (the bottles) arrive already sterilized, shrink wrapped (plastic sheeting sealing them from the air). In 1968, only 8 per cent of all port was bottled in Vila Nova de Gaia; in 1978, this proportion was 45 per cent.

Future developments will be along these lines. Steady growth and expansion in originally bottled port will lead companies either to mature more port in the Douro, thus leaving room for the preparation and bottling of the wines in Vila Nova de Gaia, or they will move outside the entreposto.

There will be further standardization of blends, apart from old tawnies of five years upwards, whilst at the same time, technically advanced companies will make more distinctive wines. Thermovinification, the technique of extracting colour from grape skins before fermentation, will play an important part in this development.

Now that refrigeration has proved itself successful after twenty years of experience in Vila Nova de Gaia, there is no reason, the Instituto do Vinho do Porto permitting, why drinkable rubies cannot be produced and enjoyed as one-year or one-and-a-half year-old wines.

The lodges

No new lodges have been built for about two hundred years. They stand, their red-tiled roofs blackened by the deposit that always forms above anything containing brandy, immobile and impressive. Cobbled streets lead to ancient gateways and, in courtyards, you will see workers in standard blue overalls, pipes stacked in rows, and triffid-type vines growing out of the granite to provide overhead shade.

But technology is encroaching on Vila Nova de Gaia. These splendid lodges, designed for maturation only, have now got to fulfil a different function. The change has been startlingly sudden, yet tradition is hard to kill, so wooden vats and pipes, cobwebs and beams overhead contrast sharply with the new technological machines and white ceramic tiles. The typical lodge complex now comprises a main office block, several or many maturing lodges, a tasting room and laboratory, a bottling hall, a tourist waiting or reception room and a dining-room. The main office block and maturing lodges vary in size and splendour from company to company.

The tasting room and laboratory are constantly being improved upon and updated. Men and women in white coats, which seem as obligatory as helmets on a building site, alternately bustle and look pensive; the tasting room, and now, even more, the laboratory, are the hubs of the business, for it is in these quiet, well-lit, clean rooms that quality and consumer acceptability are achieved or not. One traditional shipper calls this room his "kitchen" – where his devotion to his tasting art is practised with the highest professionalism. The traditional props of the wine taster are rows of tasting glasses, sawdust spittoons, plenty of daylight (walls opposite are often painted white to reflect this), serried ranks of sample bottles with coded labels, chalk to number the wines on the stone tasting table, a reference book.

How a blend is composed

The progressive port shipper is continuously experimenting. Each year produces a different set of wines to juggle with. Judicious blending is the key, especially with the more interesting quality wines. Reference samples for brands have to be matched with existing stocks. Complementary blends are called forward and blended together. They must harmonize the stringent tests of colour, bouquet and taste.

The following tasting notes show how seven wines were selected to complement each other to become the final blend for a 1977 vintage port. Equally, tawny ports must combine blends from several years, to allow flexibility for the final blend which must remain constant in its colour, bouquet and taste. All these samples were drawn for the one year, 1977, and although the head taster and his colleagues will probably make far more detailed notes on each wine on every occasion they taste it, you can see the reasons why these particular seven were selected for the final version of the establishment's 1977.

1. Quinta do Bomfim's own wine. Huge, dark wine, coarse and rather burnt, typical of the concentrated produce of the north bank of the Douro at Pinhão.

2. Big single Quinta from near Tua, very concentrated. The situation is such that the wines from here are almost more concentrated even than Sample 1.

3. Rio Torto blend of several small properties. A fresher wine than either Nos. 1 or 2. This selection is from the lower part of the Rio Torto.

4. Pinhão region above and around Quinta do Bomfim, very fresh and fine bouquet, act as foil especially to Samples Nos. 1 and 2, though in itself would produce ultimately too light a wine without great keeping qualities.

5. Lighter and more delicate wine from the upper reaches of the Rio Torto. Its lightness on the nose and freshness are again chosen to act as a foil to Nos. 1 and 2.

6. A small property in the Tavora Valley close to the Douro, the next valley downstream from the Rio Torto. One vat only of this Quinta is considered vintage worthy. A good example of the many small lotas used to make up the eventual vintage blend.

7. Made at Bomfim. Very good indeed, perhaps one of the most

balanced of all the wines shown as it is a selection made together of many small properties in the Rio Torto – Pinhão area, and therefore shows less individual characteristics than most of the preceding samples.

The final stages

The bottling hall is the one place which has seen more changes than any other aspect of the lodge complex in the last ten years. The bottling lines themselves have become more automatic, the packaging materials have improved tremendously in quality, the space needed due for expanded production has increased substantially. Forklift trucks are busy stacking cases of port destined for all international markets. Each case or carton is coded and once all documentation is ready, the shipment will be loaded onto a TIR lorry at the lodge or a ship at Leixões harbour, according to each customer's requirements.

The tourist or reception room depends on the individual company. Some companies, especially those near the quayside, actively seek out tourists to taste their produce and they have space for large groups with a bar, tables where light snacks are served and the equivalent of a shop for visitors who want to buy port at source. Others are more reticent, and some have no facilities at all.

Dining-rooms

The dining-room has been and, thankfully, still is the traditional way for the port shipper to entertain his trade and business guests. In the beginning, it was probably unwillingness to leave the office to go home and the lack of restaurants in Oporto – there is no room for them in Vila Nova de Gaia – that caused each shipper to have his own dining-room. "Come and have lunch at the lodge," is a splendid cry that invites both host and guest to look forward to a convivial break in the day. Lunch at a shipper's lodge, as with any business lunch anywhere in the world, follows a pattern. The directors and managers in charge of various aspects of the business, production, finance, sales, and their guests meet in the dining-room at around one o'clock. Usually, from six to ten are present. You might get two agents from countries as far apart as the USA and France visiting on the same day. Both are welcomed. Dry white port is always offered, other drinks are available for aperitifs. Olives and almonds act as forerunners of more substantial things to come.

Dining-rooms vary, some of them being virtually exactly as they would have been when first set up by the ancestors of the present directors – except for electric lighting and a telephone in a corner; the floorboards will be bare and polished, the furniture – usually mahogany – and the silver likewise. There may be ancestral portraits, maps and prints of the Douro on the walls and an open fire in a grate on cold winter days, often framed in an imposing marble chimney piece. Some dining-rooms overlook the river. One in particular, now refurbished in a contemporary style, has a huge picture window, through which Oporto looks like a wonderful tapestry of buildings, sky and river – and it rejoices in air-conditioning. But in all these hospitable rooms there is a feeling of isolated well-being and contentment: a 'plane may fly overhead but otherwise the only sound that penetrates will be the rhythmic bang, bang, bang of the cooper plying his task.

The wines at these lunches may come from producers elsewhere with whom the shipper enjoys friendship or even a business association but each shipper serves his own best tawny port at the end of luncheon, always decanted. There is something that is harmonious and fulfilling about drinking an old tawny in Vila Nova de Gaia; it complements the food and is often an excellent prelude to the cigar. As the port decanter hops ceremoniously around the table in a clockwise fashion, conversation and laughter exude and ripple through the air. Chairs get eased back, discussion becomes serious. This is a perfect venue for trade business and many far-reaching decisions have been taken in these dining-rooms. Laughter again – and soon it is time to go back to one's own office. There is work to be done.

V
Visiting the Region

THE DOURO VALLEY must be the most isolated of all European, if not world wine regions. It is not just that it takes three hours to get there from the nearest airport, either by car or train. When you do enter this majestic isolated country, there is virtually nowhere to taste, nowhere to eat and nowhere to stay, except, of course, in the quintas, which are all either privately owned or else the property of the port shippers themselves.

If you want to drive through France, into Spain and then through the Douro Valley on your way to Oporto (which will take two days if you do not stop), then there is nothing to stop you driving through these glorious "Portuguese Highlands". If you fly to Lisbon or Oporto and then rent a car for a few days, you will have one of the most exhilarating journeys ever, exploring the meanderings of the Douro roads and river tributaries.

The safest way to travel to the Douro is by train. The engine driver knows his way, the trains usually leave on time and the railway track follows the River Douro more closely than the roads do. Trolleys laden with beer, soft drinks and ham sandwiches are wheeled at regular intervals through the carriages. When the train stops, which is often, do not be misled by the word "*Retretes*" at each station; it is not a destination, merely the Portuguese for lavatory. There are always taxis at Regua and Pinhão, but the unshaven drivers in their green and black diesel Mercedes drive fast and furiously.

By road from Oporto

The route the port shippers take, if they do not travel on the 0750 train from Oporto, is the most direct, whilst at the same time being most scenic. Head east out of Oporto, through Valongo to Penafiel on the N15. The countryside is lush, varied and hilly. Disorganized Vinho Verde vineyards are on both sides of the road. New gaily-coloured houses, at different stages of construction, are being continuously built by Portuguese returning from abroad and spending their foreign-earned money back home. Greens and reds are predominant paint colours, grey granite blocks give a feeling of security. Tiles, in every design, are always there.

At Valongo, a mad woman in gumboots and a white helmet ceaselessly blows her whistle, directing traffic to absolutely no avail. All along this route, as on all others in Portugal, beware of children and dogs rushing into the road; beware of old men and women with loads on their heads walking along the road; beware of all cars and beware of potholes in the road.

From Penafiel, with its gargoyles and coats of arms adorning its buildings, continue on the N15 to Amarante. Midway, at Lixa, you will be able to buy beautifully embroidered linen direct from the shops where it is made on a cottage industry basis.

Amarante is a picturesque small town straddled across the River Tamega. As it is sixty kilometres from Oporto, about half-way to the Douro, it is a delightful town in which to have luncheon overlooking the river. Boats meander down the river, women do their washing on huge round boulders. The town comes alive each year on the first Saturday in June when it celebrates the feast day of its patron saint, Gonsalo, a thirteenth century priest, with a colourful agricultural fair.

The St Gonsalo Monastery dates from 1540 and the St Gonsalo bridge, which is now a national monument, is beautifully constructed in granite.

Take the Vila Real road out of Amarante, but after a few kilometres bear right on the N101 to Regua. This part of the journey takes you over the Serra do Marão (the Marão mountains), through the Quintela, and winds down to the elongated green and white town of Mesão Frio. This is dramatic countryside, and, once the Marão is crossed, the landscape being shielded from the

Atlantic, it is warmer as the descent into the Douro Valley begins. Mesão Frio, with its single street and shops in doorways huddled together, is notorious for its traffic jams, but it still remains my favourite town, after Amarante, on this route.

Since leaving Oporto, the road has been well to the north and, therefore, you are out of sight of the River Douro. But, just as somewhat forlorn hope of ever seeing it settles silently in the mind, once through Mesão Frio the grandeur of the River Douro suddenly bursts upon the unsuspecting visitor: a big wide river, with big terraced slopes is the initial impression.

Follow the N108 to Regua, which is sandwiched between the railway on the left and the river on the right. You are now truly in the Douro wine region.

Another route

The alternative route from Oporto to Regua takes about the same time, has less traffic, but much twistier roads. And by twistier roads, I mean twistier roads. Overall, the scenery is less dramatic, though more wooded. Follow the river out of Oporto on the N108. For forty-five kilometres the Douro remains more or less in view until you reach Entre-os-Rios, where some good food, including lamprey, when in season, may be found. The N210 then goes to Marco de Canaveses and the N321 winds to the town of Baião. Turning left out of Baião, the road joins the Amarante-Mesão Frio road and thence to Regua.

Starting from Lisbon

From Lisbon, the direct route to Regua takes you delightfully diagonally through the middle of northern Portugal. Drive north to Coimbra, the first capital of Portugal, and, since the seventeenth century, known as the university town, and continue on the N1 to Mealhada, famous for its suckling pig. At Mealhada, turn right along the N234 to Sta. Comba Dão and north on the N2 to Viseu, the capital of the Dão wine region. The Viseu school of painting is represented by Gaspar Vaz in the Grão Vasco Museum, and old Viseu is a charming illustration of Portuguese history. Continue north through Castro Daire to Lamego, which is an attractive, small, baroque town famed for its smoked ham. Thence to Regua.

Starting in Spain

From Galicia and north Spain, the most direct route to Regua takes you due south from the most famous smoked ham centre in Portugal, Chaves, through Vila Pouca de Aguiar to Vila Real on the N2. Vila Real is a lively town with a well-known car racing circuit. It stands at the foothills of the Serra do Marão and its most famous nearby village is, of course, Mateus, which is right on the roadside. Continue on the N2 south to Regua.

From Central Spain

From Madrid and west Spain, the road to take is fascinating in its primitive sparseness. Cross the frontier at Vilar Formoso, then the N332 goes northwards to Figueira de Castelo Rodrigo and up to Vila Nova de Foscôa. It would appear that the longer the name, the worse the road. This route is pioneering stuff – exhilarating in retrospect, terrifying when doing it. Expanses of shrubland gradually give way to terraced vineyards and, by the time you have reached S. João da Pesqueira on the N222, you are enveloped by the splendid Douro Valley. Continue west through the best vineyard area around Pinhão to Regua.

Where to stay or stop

In an area where there are no hotels or restaurants which are gastronomic either by nature or intent, standards vary and what may have been good five years ago or even last year may now have to be avoided. If you have a car, then the best places to base yourselves for one or two nights would be at the Estalagem Columabano in Regua or at the Hotel do Parque in Lamego, and explore from there.

If you want to stay in more rural surroundings, arrange to stay in one of Portugal's twenty-five state-owned pousadas. These traditionally are delightful old convents or palaces that have been bought and preserved by the State and are designed to be enjoyed by tourists. During the high season or the summer, the visitor can only stay three consecutive nights in one pousada, but during the less busy winter months, five consecutive nights are allowed. There are three such hotels just inside Portugal, if you are driving from Northern Spain, one at Caniçada, north-east of Braga, one at Bragança, and another at Miranda do Douro to the east. However, the pousada nearest the Douro Valley is just outside Amarante on the road to Vila Real. This Pousada de São Gonçalo stands in the very heart of the Serra do Marão, amidst scent- filled pinewoods. The view is spectacular as the calm is real.

The Portuguese National Tourist Offices in London and other cities are happy to supply further information, although actual bookings should be made direct with the pousadas, so get a travel agent to do this, unless you can tackle bookings for yourself.

Regua is the capital of the port district. The overseeing body, the Casa do Douro is based there; but as soon as you can, cross the bridge onto the south bank and take the road to Pinhão and beyond. This is country that demands your attention.

Quintas

A quinta in the Douro Valley is, in connotation, rather like a château in Bordeaux. It can be a magnificent, well-groomed estate, producing the finest wine, or it can be an isolated building with a farmland attached with a handful of vines nearby. The Trades Description Act has not yet rumbled these bastions of image. The word simply means a property – not necessarily a wine estate.

In the Douro Valley there are some famous quintas producing wines of the highest quality, similar to first growths in Bordeaux. These are mainly owned by the leading port shippers and thus wines are sometimes declared as vintage ports in their own right. If they are not so declared, their wines will form the base of that shipper's vintage port. In years when no vintage is declared these wines will form the base of the shipper's finest tawny ports.

Many of these quintas have been producing first-class wine for over one hundred years, some making one hundred pipes, others up to three hundred each year. Below are five of the best known. These are not lived in all the year round. Some port shippers use them more than others, but as a rule, although work continues on the vineyards throughout the year, the actual houses are only opened when the port shipper is visiting the quinta; this, of course, is something he does at regular intervals, but generally there will be several guests invited to share the excitement of the vintage and others may be invited for short stays or a lunch party during the summer. In August, however, people are usually on holiday – work goes on, but shippers (especially those with young families) will tend to be at the coast.

In former times, not having their lunches packed or their coffee flasks filled for them by loving wives, the directors used to fill their own "cantils" (wooden flasks) that they carried with them strapped across their shoulders, to sustain them through the long, hot and dusty days. The inscription on one of them indicates the contents:

> *I must have one at eleven,*
> *It's a duty that must be done.*
> *If I don't have one at eleven,*
> *Then I must have eleven at one.*

The seasonal consumption pattern of dry white port must have reached its zenith in September and October.

Quinta Boa Vista

Always linked with Offley Forrester. The sweet luscious wine produced at this quinta formed the base of Offley's celebrated vintage ports during the nineteenth century. André Simon says that the vineyards at Boa Vista were planted by Baron Forrester himself. Offley, through Sandeman, still buy the wine, but the quinta is now owned jointly by Eulalio José da Fonseca and the Seminario do Christo Rei. This Boa Vista on the north side of the Douro between Regua and Pinhão, is not to be confused with another quinta, which is in Fontelo south-east of Regua, and has the same name.

Quinta do Bomfim

Owned by the Symington family, through their company Silva and Cosens, who ship Dow port. The entrance to this fine quinta is hard by where the railway track and the bridge almost intersect in

Pinhão. The Symingtons use Bomfim both as a modern wine centre and as a home during vintage time to return to after visiting outlying farmers. The house itself was built in 1886 and was one of the first wine centres in the Douro. Its verandas and pillars give it a marvellous colonial atmosphere. Bomfim provides an excellent and friendly family estate during the year and essential at vintage time. With the expansion of the port trade in recent years, additional outdoor concrete vats have been built in many quintas to hold the wine until it is taken to Vila Nova de Gaia the following Spring. These vats, affectionately called "mamas", on account of their contours similar to breasts, are now an essential part of the Douro landscape.

Quinta do Noval

It is important to separate the actual Quinta do Noval from all the different ports shipped by Noval. The company who owns Quinta do Noval was called A. J. da Silva. They have recently changed their name to Quinta do Noval – Vinhos SARL, because Noval represented their finest wine and also because they wanted to avoid confusion with the other da Silva companies in Oporto. But they still retain the initials AJS on the glass seal of their replica eighteenth-century port bottles. However, they cannot provide all their needs just from the vineyards of Noval; like other shippers, they must buy from other farmers. The Van Zeller family look after the estate with immaculate experience and good taste. Noval, presiding over the Pinhão valley, just north of the town of Pinhão, with its wide terraces and its name elegantly etched in white on its walls, is one of the finest showpieces in the Douro Valley. The famous ungrafted *nacional* vines are still grown here. A proportion of these wines are always included in Noval's vintage port as their vinosity adds a further deeper, richer and darker dimension to the blend. The house, with its thick white walls and dark green window shutters, gives warmth in the winter and coolness in the summer. Noval is a true estate, complete with its family home, its vineyards, its lodges, houses for the estate workers and accommodation for the animals. Traditional lagars, though no longer used, stand side by side with new stainless steel fermentation tanks making up the wine centre, which Fernando Van Zeller describes as his "unfinished symphony". There is even a swimming pool cunningly built into a terrace, surrounded by vines and olive trees and serving as an additional reservoir for the winery if required. You can swim and open your mouth to the spring that supplies the pool from the mountain.

Quinta da Roêda

"If the wine district were a golden ring, Roêda would be the diamond in that ring," wrote the Portuguese poet Vega Cabral in 1865. It is Croft's quinta; a model quinta, and, thanks to Robin and Elsa Reid of Croft, over the years it has become as well known for its hospitality as for its wine. My love of the Douro Valley and thence the port trade, stems from Roêda. Some things never change. As instanced by the intrepid Charles Sellers in 1899, "When we arrived at Quinta da Roêda the barbecue suckling, the roast turkey and chicken awaited us. I strongly recommend all intending visitors to the Douro not to drink too much water: the medical men affirm that it produces intermittent fever. I think I did taste it on one occasion, but in the Douro they put it not upon the table."

Close to Bomfim, and modelled on the same lines, Roêda's entrance is on the right just before you cross over the bridge to Pinhão. Croft bought the quinta from Taylors at the turn of the century and built an Indian-tea-planter's-type bungalow in the 1920s. At one time, the original house was to be used as a breeding-place for silkworms, but this project was not successful. Today, the Reids and their guests use the bungalow, the resident staff the house.

Before cars or lorries arrived on the scene it was decidedly sensible to have your estate near the Douro, which not only provided you with natural transport but also with water.

As both the railway and the main road tend to follow the river contours in the Douro Valley, most of the big quintas now find themselves within yards of these three lifelines. Looking at Roêda from neighbouring hills, the estate looks relatively flat, but when you are climbing in between the serried vines up to the house or the frontier with the neighbouring Quinta da Roncão, you think differently.

The estate comprises a big modern wine centre which is necessary to accommodate all the grapes brought in during vintage time from farmers. The original lodge still houses evocative wooden vats of bygone vintages and the house itself offers relaxation and well-being. Even the most jet-lagged, tense businessman can relax in the Douro Valley; it is only a matter of time. All port shippers like to invite their agents from all over the world to stay at their Quinta and drink in the atmosphere. Croft is no exception.

On the Quinta, there are also offices, laboratory equipment, dormitories to sleep sixty or so men and women at vintage time, a farm still comprising chickens, turkeys, pigs, a well-tended vegetable garden, mules, olive trees and beehives. Oranges, grapefruit, almonds, figs and cork trees are also grown in abundance. In these areas it is useful to be self-sufficient.

When Croft declares a vintage, the wines from Roêda will go into Croft's vintage port. In good years, but not vintage years, Croft sometimes declares a single Quinta vintage, Quinta da Roêda. These have an elegant, flowery bouquet, which actually comes from the gum cistus flower which grows wild on the Quinta and whose scent is carried through to the grapes.

Quinta de Vargellas

Taylors bought Vargellas in 1893, when the ravages of phylloxera had reduced its output to a scanty six pipes per year. Over the years, they have restored both the vineyards and the house. In so doing they have fulfilled the hopes of Charles Sellers, who wrote in 1899, "Taylors by judicious replanting of the best parts of the Quinta hope to restore it to its former reputation". Vargellas is much closer to the Spanish frontier than the other leading quintas. As the soil gets rougher, so the grapes get hardier. As Vargellas form the base for their vintage ports, it is easy to see why Taylors always produce such a deep, intense vintage wine.

At the beginning of the eighteenth century, the Quinta Vargellas was three separate quintas. The first part, then known as Quinta do Vale, was owned by the famous Dona Antonia Ferreira and then, on her death, was left to her daughter and thereby came into the possession of the Conde de Azambuja. The Quinta de Vargellas do Meio (the middle quinta) was owned by the Carvalho Oporto family. The third part, known variously as Quinta de Vargellas de Baixo, also as Quinta de Galega and Quinta do Brito, was owned from the time of the Peninsular War until his death in 1829 by Antonio Brito e Cunho – a lively and wealthy gentleman of Oporto. He was also very active politically. Unfortunately he was on the wrong side during the Miguelite War between the two brothers and was hanged in the Praça in Oporto on 7th May 1829.

Letters have recently come to light which show that, already by this time, Quinta de Vargellas was selling as a single quinta port in London. Taylors have retained this policy in most non-vintage years.

In their sample room, I tasted bottles of port made at Vargellas in 1937, but each produced from different grape varieties. The three were Roriz, Tinta Francesa and Tinta Cão. All had developed their own character, with the Roriz being the fastest developer and most scented.

This Quinta boasts lovely, long symmetrical terraces and during the dusty summer months your car blazes a western trail through the ripening vines announcing your impending arrival. Enough time elapses for hosts to pull a cork or get the ice out of the fridge for the first welcoming drink.

Hospitality

At all these quintas, the staple drinks are a dry white port as an aperitif and an old tawny port drunk at leisure after luncheon or dinner. (However, no quinta owner is so chauvinistic or inhospitable as not to provide the necessary gin, whisky or the very good local brandy, if so desired.) Dry white port, chilled and with a slice of lime plucked from the nearest tree outside, makes an excellent aperitif. *Tapas* (to borrow the Spanish word) are always served with aperitifs, and these may include roasted almonds, black or green olives, cherry tomatoes and delicate chunks of smoked ham. The choice will vary, but one thing is certain – whatever is served will have been grown on the estate.

Although locals and visitors alike praise dry white port when lazily drinking it in the Douro, in Oporto or in the Algarve in the south, it seems to me to be one of those drinks that does not stand up to competition outside its native territory. But many countries love it, even though the British still seem to feel that port must be a red wine.

Table wines are always served with luncheon and dinner; either the dry pétillant table wines of the Minho, the Vinho Verdes which fit into a summer's day like a hand in a glove, or else the full earthy red wines from the Dão area just south of the Douro Valley, are most likely to be served. Port shippers are usually interested more in their own wine, port, than mere table wine and so due reverence does not really start until the decanter has started its circulation by the host.

Port, even old tawny port, is always decanted by port shippers in the Douro. Vintage port is seldom drunk. Some houses produce special blends of tawny port to suit the dry atmosphere. Others keep their tawnies in the Douro, having bottled them in Vila Nova de Gaia, for sufficient time to attract the magical Douro "burn" or "bake", that is so precious.

The accepted port glass is rather like a small Paris goblet. (A rounded goblet on a stem, the bowl being of at least 5½ fl. oz. capacity.) These sit happily on the white tablecloth waiting to be filled and filled again as the decanter quietly and conversationally goes round the table. Cigarettes and cigars are never offered before the first glass of port has been appreciated. Ladies do tend to leave the dinner table after a while, though I suspect not before they are sure there is another decanter in the drawing-room.

A Douro farm

In addition to these showplace working quintas, there are many others carefully positioned throughout the Douro Valley. Some are no more than farms at the end of a track. Port or table wine is their sole commercial life; their remaining crops are grown to feed themselves. These farmers tend to be old now; their sons and daughters have left the valley for "progress" in the towns and cities. With their black hats, stubble chin, and baggy clothes they have a wealth of knowledge about the countryside and the wine it provides.

To ensure that the vats (*balseiros*) into which the newly made wine is put are up to each port shipper's standard, the port shipper visits each farmer and checks each vat. In the early 1960s, I witnessed such an event. We clambered out of the car to broad smiles. Ushered into the house, we were proffered a glass of sixty-year-old tawny port that had never left the farm on which it was made. Deliciously tawny and burnt ... and yes, we would like another one, please. Meanwhile, the farmer's wife was cooking in the huge open fireplace with two hanging black cauldrons sizzling away on the open fire fuelled with vine roots. No oven and no electricity. Soon we went to inspect the vats.

The tiny door at the front of one vat was removed, we banged the outside of the vat to shake up the inside and put our heads in. A marvellous tartaric and tannic aroma from previous vintages emanated. Initials okaying the vat were inscribed thereon in chalk. Two more similar vats were inspected. Many mutual "*obrigados*" (thank-yous) were exchanged, caps doffed and we returned to our car. Quality control was over for another year.

This painstaking and time-consuming exercise was necessary, as I have also visited a farmer, who, on removing the tiny door, appeared just as startled as we certainly were when a clutch of clacking chickens appeared from the vat. However, this ancient yet successful form of quality control is now rapidly giving way to the influence of wine centres, where proper technical controls can function on each shipper's home ground.

Several quintas are owned by absentee landlords – mostly wealthy Portuguese industrialists, who may come from Oporto or Lisbon. These estates are usually well cared for and the wine produced is sold to the same shipper year after year. Other quintas are owned by large-scale farmers, who like other farmers, are constantly improving and enlarging their property, making it more efficient and profitable.

Places of Interest

The best time to visit the vineyards is whenever suits you, but from May to September the weather is pleasantest. In the winter, the countryside is bare and there is not much work going on. In the spring, the vineyards are green and busy developing and in the summer they are a brownish purple. There is always a calmness, a stillness throughout the Douro, which makes it so special.

Remember that from the beginning of July until the end of September it is likely to be really hot and, as the roads wind about, some travellers may find a lengthy excursion tiring. Plan to make several stops, especially if you have children with you and do not count on finding anywhere to get a drink or snack outside the towns; take a vacuum flask with a cold drink and some fruit or light refreshments if you need to eat on time.

If you are staying in the Douro, you should be prepared against the local mosquitos – they do not touch the locals but they thrive on new blood. Remember, too, that you need to take precautions against the Douro sun – creams and lotions are not always easy to find up country.

If, by happy fortune, you are at Regua with a car and have several spare hours or even days in front of you, this is an itinerary which would help you understand and appreciate the countryside which produces port. If you are staying at Vila Real or Lamego, then come to Regua before going on into the outer wilds. Take no notice of distances on signposts: these will be correct, but the roads are so twisting and turning that you are never able to adjust mentally to the averages you are achieving. Time taken over certain distances is difficult to calculate. Signposts are generally good and clear.

If you come from Vila Real, first of all pay a visit to the Mateus Palace at Mateus, three kilometres to the east on the N322; the magnificent building which is on the wine's label can be seen in real life in all its rich baroque charm.

Regua is a crossroads. It is where the city mentality meets the country mentality. The Casa do Douro is here; it is here therefore where quantities and price are discussed in every bar and café. It is a town full of peasants trying to be businessmen, where dogs bark continually and everyone else gossips endlessly. For years Regua had a maze-like one-way system for cars that even Hampton Court would have disapproved. The railway station is the biggest in the Douro; it is always a hive of activity and the train running between Oporto and the Spanish frontier stops a full fifteen minutes at Regua as though atoning for its slowness.

The countryside west of Regua is lush and generous. This is good farmland, but it produces quantity rather than quality. As Sarah Bradford says in *The Story of Port*,

> "port, however, is a paradoxical wine: the lusher the vineyard, the more moderate the climate, the worse the port. Contrary to what one would expect, the high quality port grape is a

miserable looking object, small, round and dull black like a
miniature squash ball. To find it you have to travel up river,
beyond the tributary of the Corgo which joins the Douro at
Regua, to the Cima Corgo district, where the soil is poorer, the
climate hotter and the rainfall scarcer."

Leave Regua station, cross the bridge to the south bank and take
the N222 to Pinhão. Once past the River Corgo you are officially in
the Cima (or upper) Corgo region. In a few minutes you will see an
enormous dam across the River Douro, which is one of several being
built principally to generate hydro-electricity. Pause for a moment
then to peer over and look at the dramatic new level of the river to
the east: the latter represents the old Douro, full of rapids and rocks,
the former represents the new Douro, a peaceful lake. The dam
engineers decided to leave the single rail track where it was, on the
north side of the river, but the new water level meant that the old
road disappeared (hoorah) and so a new one was built higher up.

As you look along the road, there are tapestries of vineyards.
White farmhouses perch on the occasional flat ground as though
they are sentry boxes watching over the growing vines. Just before
you reach Pinhão, look across the river to Quinta la Rosa; flanked
by cypress trees, la Rosa, owned by the Feuerheerd family for many
generations, has long been a haven of conviviality. The late Claire
Bergqvist held court there for many years, and it is now owned by her
son, Tim. Beyond la Rosa is the delightful Quinta do Vale da Foz,
owned by the Cálem family and round the corner is Quinta do Eira
Velha. The romantic sounding Eira Velha belongs to the Newman
family, who at vintage time fly the Union Jack, the Portuguese flag
and the old Newman Newfoundland Shipping House flag, because
centuries ago they used to do much trade in *bacalhau* there. The
production is now bought by Cockburn's, who in 1978 declared
Quinta do Eira Velha as a single quinta vintage port.

Crossing the iron bridge into Pinhão is a symbolic way of saying
that you are now entering the very best vineyard areas in the Douro
Valley. Pinhão is like nowhere else. Women are constantly washing
their clothes in the river, the azulejos tiles greeting you at the railway
station are as remarkable as they are unique; the town has a petrol
station, a shop where you can buy films for your camera – remember
there is almost always a thin blue haze in the Douro which often

inhibits photographs – and one cobbled street which is constantly being dug up and put back together again.

Keep going up through the village on the N323, alongside the River Pinhão, one of the larger tributaries of the Douro, and soon you will reach Quinta do Noval on the right, with a long arcade of vines leading round the mountain to the house. Below, the road winds past Vale de Mendiz, the Sandeman house, not called a quinta as they have no land there. Up in the hills is Celeiros, where Sandeman have a large impressive wine-making centre. Sandeman, who started advertising back in the 1920s, were pioneers of the wine centre system in the 1960s; their large wine centre near Regua houses fifteen thousand pipes in wood in one lodge. It makes sense to take advantage of the open space in the Douro away from the cramped quarters in Vila Nova de Gaia.

If you return and go back on the other side of the Pinhão valley, the road winds its way to Alijó, outside the demarcated port region. Continuing on the N212, you rejoin the Douro where its tributary, the River Tua, also joins it. On the right is Quinta dos Malvedos, a fine estate, also situated near road, railway and the river. Following the railway line, you come to Tua, the preserve of Cockburn. Originally bought by them as a convenient centre from which to control their fine wine purchase in this area, the quinta, known as Quinta dos Ingleses (the English Quinta) to the locals, has recently been extended into a wine centre. Cockburn's main wine centre, however, is just outside Regua. Cockburn directors used to take vintage time so seriously that women were not encouraged to visit Tua during this period but this rule is gradually being relaxed, to the delight of all – or so I am told.

Beyond Tua is once famous Quinta do Zimbro, which used to belong to Silva & Cosens and above is the delightfully rural village of Ribalonga. For generations, the families who farm in this valley have sold their wines to the same port shippers.

This is really the farthest east you can drive by car in the wine district, where, of course, the vineyards cannot be more than five hundred metres above sea level. Above this level, there are patches of wheat and other crops. The train crosses over to the south bank at Ferradosa. Your car must turn back to Regua or Vila Real.

To explore the south bank of the Douro and the River Torto, recross the bridge at Pinhão. Passing the entrance of Quinta das

Carvalhas, one of the largest quintas in the Cima Corgo, follow the N222 round the mountain to the left and take the signpost to São João da Pesqueira (St John the Fisherman). Carvalhas is a big, steep-sloping quinta facing north, almost opposite Roêda. It is owned by Manuel Silva Reis, of the Companhia Velha; apart from the large working quinta down by the river, Manuel Silva Reis has built a circular house on top of the hill. From a distance this looks like a weather station, but is in fact a comfortable home.

Leaving the Douro, you enter the classic majesty of the River Torto. Folds of vineyards stretch out and up and along, tall, dark cypress trees and silvery olive trees break up this rich pageant of rolling solid vineyards. The beauty of Ramos Pinto's Quinta Bom Retiro gives way to other quintas intertwined between the vines. Awesome, yet real; majestic, yet simple.

Once you have gained height, the Douro is in sight again and, from just beyond Quinta do Ventoselo there is a magnificent view of Quinta da Roêda and Roncão, whose production Delaforce buy. Then there is Quinta do Roriz, which produced so many fine vintage ports in the last century.

After Ervedoza do Douro you reach São João da Pesqueira, one of the most charming villages in this primitive wilderness. Like all Douro villages, it has its share of scruffy bars and cafes, small children running all over the place and older folk who stand and talk or sometimes just stand. São João da Pesqueira has a most picturesque prison in the attractive main square. I was there once having an animated conversation with a prisoner when one of our party threw him a five pence piece. Being on the first floor, the prisoner caught it. We thought it would look good on expenses – "Tipping prisoner – five pence". There is a small newish hotel where a brief stay could be made and there are shops where you can buy picnic provisions.

Just outside the town, several handsome baroque buildings are to be seen, including the country mansion of the Marquês de Soveral, at one time ambassador to the Court of St James's and friend of Edward VII.

Less than ten minutes from São João da Pesqueira is São Salvador do Mundo. This is a strange, incongruous place. There are little chapels forming a "sacred way" escorting you to the top,

Factory House, Oporto
(exterior).

Factory House: one of two identical dining-rooms, each seating
forty-six people.

Factory House: the main
staircase.

(*below*) Factory House: the
ballroom.

Joseph James Forrester (1809–1862), pioneer, cartographer, historian, and wine merchant.

Instituto do Vinho do Porto: museum room.

Douro vineyard, the vines juxtaposed with olive trees.

A typical bunch of port wine grapes.

Quinta da Roêda, before and after the recent vineyard plantations on what had been scrubland.

Harvest time in the Douro Valley: the grapes are picked.

where there is a pagan-Christian shrine. Each of the little chapels contains models of holy scenes with animated figures, lovingly carved and decorated. Devils' footprints are to be found on a large smooth rock.

VI
Port Shippers' Lodges

THE STEEP, TWISTING cobbled streets climbing up from the south bank of the River Douro act as boundaries between all the port houses neatly juxtapositioned in the entreposto – Vila Nova de Gaia. It is as though the whole of Gaia is a jigsaw puzzle of which each shipper's lodge is an irregular section. The steep granite walls are separated by frighteningly angled cobbled ways alive with buses, TIR lorries, green-topped Mercedes diesel taxis, cars and the inevitable motor-cycles minus exhaust pipes. The ox-drawn carts of former times were infinitely preferable, albeit slower.

Even though the mode of transport has changed dramatically over the years, the average Portuguese have not. They still honour the dead by almost always wearing mourning black and the women carry all kinds of goods on their heads – whether the load be a sack of potatoes or several bottles of wine, this is a custom that has stood the test of time. The Portuguese will put anything on her head, either directly (wedged on a kind of coiled flat turban) or on one of the flat wicker basket trays, which may sway but are never upset. Some years ago, when, in an attempt to "educate" the peasantry, legislation empowered the police to fine anyone crossing the – then – sole bridge between Oporto and Gaia barefoot, it was quite usual to see a woman take down one sandal or clog from the basket on her head before starting to walk across, leaving the other in the basket and thus satisfying the law!

The occasional *barco rabelo* remains moored alongside the quay in Gaia, usually bearing the insignia of one of the port houses, because such boats are really publicity devices these days. But all commercial ships use the purpose-built port of Leixões, four miles to the north.

There are now two bridges across the river from Oporto, leading to Vila Nova de Gaia rather as in a pincer movement. The visitor may turn left after crossing the new Ponte Arrábida, built in 1963, or immediately right, after negotiating the lower part of the double-decker iron bridge, called Dom Luis I, built in 1886 (the bridge traditionally featured in photographs and posters of Oporto, joining it to Gaia). The tourist will then be confronted with numerous signs announcing the whereabouts of at least twenty port houses: many will simply say "Welcome", others will indicate that they offer tastings, a few will have a message in French, an indication that France has been the leading export market for port for the past twenty years. Each sign is different: some are new, some tatty, some small, some big, some indicate familiar names, others firms little known to the outsider. But one thing is definite: along this quarter mile of quayside are all the port shippers, with a backdrop of Oporto across the river. The lengthy, red-tiled roofs, housing warehouses two hundred years old that are tilted at crazy angles, shelter the head offices of the port trade.

The complexes that make up this area need examining and understanding if the visitor is to appreciate the legacy which many of these old-established companies have inherited and which needs to be transformed into modern commerce if the firms are to survive the rigours of twentieth-century competition. To envisage the "cheek by jowlness" of the port shippers' entreposto, which covers about two hundred hectares of uneven, cobbled slopes, it is as though all whisky producers were based in Aberdeen instead of being spread throughout the Highlands and other regions of Scotland, or as if all the Bordeaux châteaux wishing to ship their wine had to send it to one demarcated area just outside Bordeaux, where all the head offices of every company had to be located.

When all port was exported in pipes, the location of the shippers in Gaia was in many ways ideal. The pipes of matured wine were rolled from the lodges and loaded onto an ox cart; the oxen then teetered down the hill to the quay and there offloaded; the pipes were then rolled up a plank into the waiting ship. Later, they were hoisted aboard by a crane, but the principle remained the same. Now the vast majority of port, whether exported in bulk or in bottle, is shipped in containers, either from the port of Leixões or direct from the shipper's lodge. Containerization basically means that a sufficient volume of liquid or number of cases can be put on a lorry or into a ship which can be sealed until the destination is reached. In this way, transport costs are minimized and theft is lessened.

The usefulness of Gaia's geographical position has thus been superseded by economic events. Although one or two of the more progressive companies have applied for and, after several years, have received permission from all the relevant authorities concerned to move out of the entreposto, none have so far taken this dramatic and costly step – but doubtless it will happen.

Firms to visit

Most of the shippers open their lodges to visitors and a number have multi-lingual guides to show people round. In some, the lodge will have a public tasting room or reception area where wines can be sampled and, sometimes, olives and nuts may be served. In general, the lodges are open from the early summer until after the vintage except, of course, at weekends and on public holidays. It is wise to make an appointment if you want to see round a particular lodge, unless you take part in a pre- arranged tour. The normal procedure is to contact the national importer of the relevant company well in advance of a visit. As it is sometimes difficult to be precise about times or even dates when on holiday, it is probably wisest to have the wine merchant or national representative back home send a message to the effect that So-and-So will be in the area at such-and-such a time and will then telephone to make a specific appointment. This, of course, is for visitors who do have some serious interest in port and may need some specific information. But, whereas trade visitors and groups of wine lovers are welcomed to Gaia in hundreds every year, consumer visitors are received in the thousands, most of them coming from France and the U.K., as well as from Portugal.

The best times of the year to visit Oporto or, rather, Gaia, and possibly the Douro as well are late spring and early autumn. The holiday months of July and August are popular of course, but it is then very hot indeed. Although most lodges will be open for visitors in August, the shippers themselves are usually on holiday then; so, if you want to see anyone particular, this is not a good time to arrive.

If you can read something of the history of the port shippers before visiting Gaia, your enjoyment will be much enhanced (see Appendix i on p. 149). Anyone who then wants to find out more about port can do no better than to visit a shipper's lodge, gaze in awe at millions of litres slumbering in oak vats or pipes, taste the product and then buy whichever they particularly like, either direct from the shipper or when they are back home.

Unless whoever shows you round when you visit a lodge makes it obvious that they expect a tip, do not offer anything except thanks. Someone on the staff of the firm will naturally not expect to be tipped but occasionally a guide allocated to a party on a tour of several places of interest may indicate that some solid form of thanks will be appreciated. If you meet any of the executives of the firm it is, of course, a pleasant gesture to write a note of thanks afterwards. By the way, when you visit a lodge this is an opportunity to make inquiries about any excursion you plan in the Douro Valley; some firms may be able to make an appointment for you to see a winery and something of the estate, although the best way is to take a picnic and simply explore the country. But do be punctilious about keeping to any time that has been arranged – otherwise somebody may be waiting for you when they should be working. Get the telephone number and then, if you are delayed in arriving, you can either ring up or get some helpful garage or café to make the call and explain the situation – remember, up-country, language can be a real barrier.

Charles Sellers' book *Oporto, Old & New, being a historical record of the Port Wine Trade and a tribute to British Enterprise in the North of Portugal* was published in 1899; this three-hundred page bible of the trade contains twenty-one chapters on the major port companies at that time. Since then many of the older, smaller concerns have been taken over or simply disappeared from view; the companies that have emerged or been developed since then are on a sounder commercial basis. They have gradually been building up brand loyalty among their customers rather than relying on supplying unmarked blends, as in the time when individual and often small-scale merchants would simply send along so many dozens of "the usual" port to mess stewards, club secretaries and retail customers, whose cellars rarely received any port actually labelled with the name of its maker.

Each major shipper today will have printed leaflets or brochures giving basic details of the thread of history that runs through their companies. Some of the books listed in Appendix i will fill out the picture of major houses. Two leading shippers, Warre and Croft, recently celebrated their tercentenaries and each produced a hard-backed book about themselves. Here I have tried to help the potential visitor to visualize what is signified by some of the great names in port, maybe while he or she is sitting at home by the fire with a glass of old tawny port at hand. My comments are designed to indicate the individual characteristics that mark each company's premises, rather than to give a complete historical or business account. But remember – the port shippers themselves are as close-knit as the entreposto in Gaia; they close ranks with traditional ease, and all of them are equally at home in Portugal or England, in Portuguese or English – a fine example of "England's oldest alliance".

The following companies are some of the most instructive and interesting lodges to visit:

A. A. Cálem

This family firm, established in 1859, is one of the leading Portuguese shippers. Perched right on the edge of the quay nearest to the double-decker bridge, Cálem's lodges are always devastatingly affected whenever the Douro floods, which is quite frequently, in spite of the dams that have recently been built. Frighteningly high chalk lines on the walls mark the major floods of 1909, 1962, 1978 and 1979.

Cálem's initial business was to ship Portuguese table wine to Brazil. To avoid empty boats coming back to Portugal, they used to bring back wood for casks and this resulted in the building up of a cooperage company, which in turn led to them storing and maturing port. They thus became port shippers by accident rather than design.

Cálem have a unique tradition of maintaining a house and office across the river, on the Oporto side, in addition to the mandatory offices and lodge in Vila Nova de Gaia; the endearing part of this custom is that the house is passed on to and is the responsibility of whoever is the head of the company at that time.

Following floods and a major fire some years ago, Cálem's lodge is now a blend of old and new; port samples are still carried on wooden trays on the heads of blue-overalled workers, empty cartons are transported from one end of the lodge to the other by an elaborate device that reminds me of some Italian ski-lifts. Cálem, like other shippers, suffer from lack of space and one of their separate lodges, sited on the left just after you cross the double-decker bridge, is literally a wooden extension from the side of a cliff. The wooden floors, honouring Cálem's antecedents, are made from cut-up staves of casks; goats stand tethered just outside during the São João festivities in mid-June (St John the Baptist's day, which is June 24th); yet side by side with these traditional relics are the stainless steel and white-tiled areas essential for maintaining the quality wines they produce.

Cockburn Smithes

If you want to see a pipe being made in the traditional way, follow the signs to the Cockburn lodge. A pipe takes an hour to make and will last forty years – the same duration as a vine. Great, square stacks of wooden staves, matured by weathering for four years, are piled high to the ceiling. The experienced coopers use numbered staves, each one fitting exactly to its neighbour, and iron rings to hold the staves in place. Steam softens the wood, then the fiery furnace dries it; a fire is lit inside the newly assembled staves and the heat pulls them together and the final iron hoop can be placed in position and the head staves fitted. Each separate piece of a cask has a separate name. It is an experience to watch and typifies the contact that each of these lodges enjoys between the old and the new.

Cockburn Smithes is a great and progressive port company. They have come a long way since they were founded in 1815 by Robert Cockburn. In 1899 they warranted less than two pages in *Oporto Old and New*. Doubtless this was because at that time the firm was a relative newcomer to Oporto and the port trade in comparison with some of the older established companies.

As with other firms, the name of the company changed with the current partners. Charles Sellers records:

> In the following year, 1848, Mr. John Smithes was admitted into partnership, the style becoming Messrs. Cockburn, Smithes & Co., as at present. During his long residence in Porto,

Mr. Smithes was one of the most popular men in the place. I believe I am correct in saying that he came from Lancashire. His brother, Mr. Henry Smithes, was long and honourably known as one of the resident partners in London.

The descendants of these two respected families, Cockburn and Smithes, ran the company for over one hundred years. The company has been owned by Harveys of Bristol since 1962.

The Cockburn lodge complex is amongst the largest. It is different from other lodges in that the recent partners of Cockburn's, all great characters in their way, decided to use pink instead of a white-wash to paint the outside of their buildings. Inside the lodges, you are immediately aware of the busy quiet, for maturing wine makes no noise.

Outside, the rumbling of traffic and honking of horns provide the main distractions. Some of the doors are very small as, when Cockburn's acquired the adjacent Martinez Gassiot company, it was, as it still is, illegal to move pipes of port from one lodge to another, so these intercommunicating doors are smaller than the width of a pipe.

Croft

Croft have recently celebrated their tercentenary, being one of the oldest companies, established in 1678. The Croft family came from Yorkshire and by the eighteenth century had become well-established in Oporto. John Croft wrote his famous *Treatise on the Wines of Portugal* in 1788; his son, also John, was created a baronet on the advice of the Duke of Wellington, as the former had fed the latter with vital information regarding movements of French troops entering Spain during the Peninsular War; the late Percy Croft, who died in 1935, uttered the immortal words: "Any time not spent drinking port is a waste of time."

As is natural when a colony is formed, there was a certain amount of intermarrying amongst the established members. The first Sir John Croft married a Miss Warre, and their son and heir had no less than six sons and nine daughters, thus creating a firm marital base for the expatriate port shippers.

One of Croft's earlier managers was Mr J. R. Wright. Again, Charles Sellers: "No merchant was more esteemed than Mr Wright.

He was a thorough Englishman." He may well have been, but unfortunately, that did not prevent him from losing an arm during the Civil War between Dom Pedro and Dom Miguel. Nor did that prevent him from announcing that Croft's would not declare the 1868 vintage, as he had just ridden up to the Douro and found the grapes shrunken and parched by the heat. On his arrival back in Oporto, he announced his decision; what he did not know was that fine rain had begun to fall in the Douro, which enabled the 1868 vintage to be near perfect. Mr Wright, being the thorough Englishman that he was, did not go back on his word. Instead, he made an exceptional 1869 vintage and had the field to himself. This shows the communications gap that existed for so long in the port trade world.

Croft and Company has long been owned, since 1911, by Gilbeys, now absorbed into International Distillers and Vintners. The catapulting from the traditional to the modern has been keenly felt at Croft's: there is now a first-class tourist room where visitors can see a film and taste several different qualities of port in the relaxed atmosphere of a two hundred year old lodge. The one hundred and thirty-six metre Terreirinho lodge is the longest port lodge in full operation in Vila Nova de Gaia – it would take the fastest runner in the world fifteen seconds to run from end to end – and, again, the clinking of glass in the bottling line and the coming and going of TIR lorries are in sharp contrast to the shafts of light that squeeze through tiny windows, spearing unsuspecting casks and dusty floors alike. The necessary tools for modern production, such as filtering plants and refrigeration tanks, are installed neatly alongside rows and rows of pipes of port. Each cask is marked in chalk to give it an identity: VT (vinho tinto) means red port; VB (vinho branco) means white port. The year is indicated and the vineyard, such as RDA (Roêda).

Croft's lodges, with their many different levels, are some of the most picturesque. They cover ten acres of ground and house an imposing granite office block. The inevitable man in blue overalls guiding the inevitable plastic pipes from one wooden pipe to another reflects the timeless care taken in producing quality wines. Some of the immense vats made of Brazilian mahogany are dedicated to past and present directors of the company, indicated by shining brass plaques. Some visitors believe that the contents of the vat belong to the person whose name is inscribed on the outside; unfortunately, I can assure you that this is not the case!

Delaforce

The Delaforce lodges are interesting to the visitor who wants to see a model traditional lodge complex with an efficient, though not extravagant, operation all under one roof. The floor levels vary with practically every step. Many of the floors are still laid with wooden staves that swell and rise in the winter and contract in the summer, the idea being to soften the impact against the pipes when they were rolled around the lodge from one resting place to another. Fork-lift trucks now do this work, but the floors remain. Pipes were cleaned in the old days by inserting a chain through the bung-hole and then rocked from side to side on a raised wooden support. Again, this method of cleaning has ceased to be economical, but the support remains, as a testament to this ancient practice.

The Huguenot Delaforces originally came from France in 1685, at the time of the revocation of the Edict of Nantes. They passed through Holland to England and the founder of the firm started the company in Oporto in 1868. A hundred years later, Delaforce was acquired by International Distillers and Vintners. Their leading brand, delightfully portraying the religious enjoying wine, is aptly called "His Eminence's Choice".

Ferreira

One of the most intriguing port companies to visit, from an historical point of view, is Ferreira. Formed in 1751, the company has been and, I hope, will always be renowned for two reasons. First, for the quality of their wines and second, for the romantic, yet tragic, inter-twining of the two most dominant characters of their day – Dona Antonia Adelaide Ferreira, born in 1810, and the ubiquitous Baron Joseph James Forrester, born one year earlier. Without the brilliant, energetic Forrester and the wealthy, idolized Dona Antonia, whose first husband, Charles Sellers, delightfully ascribes "to him the Portonians owe the elementary notion of paving streets", the history pages of the port trade would be considerably duller.

The day was May 12th, 1862. Forrester, together with the cook from the Hotel de Paris in Oporto were to lunch with Dona Antonia and others at Quinta de Vargellas, now owned by Taylor's. So keen was he to keep his luncheon date that he took with him a smaller boat than was wise. His own larger boat was out of service. The smaller boat could not withstand the swirling rapids at the Cachão de Valeira, it overturned and the great man drowned, Dona Antonia and the other ladies all being saved by the buoyancy of their crinolines, which enabled them to float to safety. Forrester's body was never found and it is possible that he was wearing a money belt, holding the wages of his workers.

The emu is Ferreira's trademark and a giant white statue of this strange bird may be seen outside their offices. In addition to entertaining probably more visitors than anyone else in Vila Nova de Gaia (around fifty thousand each year) Ferreira also run boat trips up and down the Douro for a nominal charge. This is an excellent idea and a useful way of getting a different view of both Oporto and Vila Nova de Gaia. The compact motor boat only operates during the summer months, but the excursion is well worthwhile.

Ferreira is still a family-owned company. The visitor may be confused when he hears the name Ferreirinha; it is the same company, but such is the quiet popularity of this family firm through the generations that the diminutive form of the name is often used with affection.

Graham

The first lodge that you pass coming from the new Arrábida Bridge is Graham's. The position of the lodge affords a marvellous view up river and in the lodge itself are some huge old vats, each named after a particular rank or position. For instance, there are highly polished plaques with such emboldened descriptions as "The Emperor", "The Ambassador" writ deep. Whenever a holder of that office visits Graham's, his name is added to the roll call.

Graham's was originally a successful textile concern. They came into the wine trade, it is claimed, because they had a bad debt in wine. They never regretted the move, and built up a fine reputation for producing quality ports. The first recorded shipment was of twenty-seven pipes made by Mr John Graham in 1826.

The Graham family maintained their strong Scottish connections by keeping an office in Glasgow for many years. They also decided, as did other family concerns, that they should own an estate as a base for operations as well as pleasure in the Douro. So they bought

Quinta dos Malvedos, close to the Spanish frontier. It is interesting to note that many port families either originated from Scotland or the North of England. Only such sturdy venturers could enjoy the hilly desolate countryside, akin to the Highlands of Scotland.

Graham's was recently bought by the Symington family and so is now absorbed into the Dow & Warre group of companies. Each, however, retains its separate style.

A. J. da Silva

The company which ships Noval port, A. J. da Silva, do not generally receive visitors in Vila Nova de Gaia. This company, founded in 1813, has for many years concentrated their development, not in Vila Nova de Gaia, but at their splendid Quinta do Noval near Pinhão in the Douro. By 1983 they aim to be ready to show visitors around this beautiful estate and they will, thus, probably become the first shippers to combine all their operations – buying, producing, maturing and bottling – in the Douro.

A. J. da Silva remained entirely in the hands of the da Silva family until 1920, when Antonio da Silva Junior's son-in-law, Luis Vasconcellos Porto, was admitted to the partnership. Luis Porto developed Quinta do Noval into one of the Douro's show pieces with its long, white terraced walls so elegantly contoured. His two grandsons are now carrying on the fine work that he started.

Their best known port is L.B., instantly recognizable by the white silk-screened lettering on the dumpy, traditionally shaped bottle. So as to capitalize on their magnificent quinta and not to be confused with the other Portuguese port-shippers, C. da Silva, since 1908 da Silva have always shipped their vintage ports under the Noval label.

Guimarãens

The firm of Guimarãens was originally called Fonseca, Monteiro & Co. However, it was not until Manuel Pedro Guimarãens acquired the business in 1822 that it came on to a proper commercial footing. The Guimarãens came from Braga, but during the Peninsular War Manuel Pedro Guimarãens sought refuge in England and married an English lady. Charles Sellers concedes that their three sons who all went into the business were "essentially Englishmen, although of Portuguese descent on their father's side, they had been born and educated in England".

The Guimarãens took the name Fonseca from the original firm's name and shipped all their vintage and now other ports under this label, maybe because it was easier to pronounce and was old established. In 1948, the Yeatman family of Taylor Fladgate bought the firm. As with so many other takeovers in the port world, each house retains its own lodges and style, to keep customers and preserve tradition.

Ramos Pinto

One of the most visitor-orientated shippers is Ramos Pinto. Also right on the waterfront, housed in a splendid yellow building built in 1708, this company offers the visitor who may be short of time a synopsis of the inside of a lodge, so he can get the feel. Next door, welcomed by their evocative pre-war posters, he may enjoy a range of ports in pleasant, comfortable surroundings.

Ramos Pinto, founded by Adriano Ramos Pinto in 1880, have always maintained consistent quality in their ports, based on Bom Retiro, their centrally positioned quinta in the Douro.

Sandeman

Sandeman and their trade mark, the Don, are inseparable. The Don celebrated his fiftieth anniversary in 1978. The port trade should be always grateful to the partners of Sandeman in the 1920s because it was they who first had the courageous foresight actually to advertise port. Sandeman's thus had a head start on all the other shippers, which explains why today Sandeman port can be found all over the world.

Founded in London in 1790 by George Sandeman, the company was run by his descendants until Seagram bought them out in 1979. It is traditionally one of the largest shipping companies in Vila Nova de Gaia and occupies impressive premises on the waterfront which were designed by Consul Whitehead. They too have suffered severely over the years from flooding and have kept the dreaded white lines to prove it – 1825, 1853, 1860, 1909, 1962, 1966, 1978 and 1979.

Their lodges are big, full of the traditional scissor construction roof beams; yet there is always that great contrast between the old and the new. One moment you can see a pipe being hauled up to another floor by hand, such is the pressure on space; the next, you are confronted with a battery of gleaming, modern refrigeration tanks, installed to maintain highest quality controls.

As if to demonstrate that you do not have to own your own vineyards to succeed, it was only in 1974 that Sandeman actually became their own vineyard owners. They now also have four wine centres in the Douro, at Pacheca, Celeiros, Riba Tua and Pocinho. Visitors are welcome at these if they contact Sandeman's in London or Oporto first, so that the necessary arrangements can be made.

Charles Sellers opens his chapter on Sandeman & Co. with: "I have great pleasure in being able to place before my many readers the history of the Sandeman family which has given to Great Britain brave soldiers and sailors and distinguished men in some of the highest offices of our Empire City."

They also produced a family magazine "The Clan"; George Sandeman the founder was known in the office as "Old Cauliflower" on account of his white wig, and his son, Alfred, was at one time "a most successful squatter in Australia". Colonel John Glas Sandeman invented the penny-in-the-slot machine, as well as taking part in the charge of the Heavy Brigade at Balaclava.

The first George Sandeman started a wine cellar with a £300 loan from his father. He traded for some time at Tom's Coffee House in Cornhill in the City of London. During the eighteenth century it was the custom for City merchants to do business in London's many coffee houses in the same way as the Factory in Oporto became the centre for transactions between businessmen. George Sandeman decided to specialize in sherry and port. Sandeman 1790 was the first vintage port he declared. By 1792 he was representing the sherries of James Duff of Cadiz and in 1809 started shipping Madeira into Britain. In the meantime he travelled extensively in Spain and Portugal and the firm even ran their own wine clipper, the *Hoopoe*, between the Peninsula and the east coast ports of England until 1875, when they sold her.

Along the way, Sandeman acquired Robertson's who in turn had taken over the business of Rebello Valente in 1881. Their other subsidiaries, Diez, and Baron Forrester's old company, Offley Forrester, are jointly owned with the French company who make St Raphaël. Offley Forrester occupy different premises, including the splendid "Lodge of the Eagles" which they have recently renovated.

Offley Forrester

The original firm of Offley Forrester dates back to 1761. The Offleys were a distinguished family, boasting a Lord Mayor of London, Sir Thomas Offley, in 1556. The first Forrester to join the firm was Joseph James Forrester's uncle in 1803: his nephew joined him in 1831 and this gifted, far-sighted man would have surely advanced his company along the most progressive lines had not he died at fifty-two years of age in the Cachão rapids (see page 89).

Taylor

Taylors 1927 . . . This great vintage port from the firm Taylor, Fladgate and Yeatman epitomizes to me all that is best in a vintage port. Taylor have always commanded quality, loyalty and high prices for their vintage ports. They now use this expertise in the production of their Late Bottled Vintage Reserve Ports.

Job Bearsley was the founder of the firm in 1692 which, by the addition of Joseph Taylor in 1816, John Fladgate in 1837 and Morgan Yeatman in 1844, finally emerged in its present-day form. Between 1692 and 1844 there were no less than twenty-one changes in the company name; one of these, Webb, Campbell, Gray & Cano, which lasted from 1808 to 1813, is interesting because for the first and only time to date an American, Joseph Cano, was admitted to the partnership in a port company. It was a shrewd move because, as a neutral during the Peninsular War, he was able to try to keep regular exporting services open in the face of the invading French led by Marshal Soult.

Just after the Phylloxera ravages, Taylor bought Quinta da Vargellas, one of the more remote but beautiful quintas in the Douro, close to Spain.

The firm happily combine tradition with progress. Huge glass doors with their "4 x x" trademark embossed in red lead to their traditional lodges. The visitor can still see the volume measurement in almudes and canadas (see glossary) as opposed to litres, on key pipes. The respective measurements are:

1 pipe (534.2 litres) = 21 almudes (each 25.4 litres)
= 252 canadas (each 2.1 litres)

I was told the explanation for these seemingly strange volume measurements. One oxcart could pull a pipe; an *almude* could be carried on one's head; and a *canada* was the optimum measure that a man could drink!

Taylors, as it is always known in its shortened form, represents the spirit of independence in the same way that the other group of independent companies, controlled by the Symington family, represent the spirit of family independence.

Warre

Warre boast the largest wooden vat in Vila Nova de Gaia. Measured at 2½ million glasses of port, representing two hundred and forty-four pipes, it allows fourteen glasses to the bottle. Average rather than overgenerous. It is a most impressive sight and the visitor can also see, by the use of colour shades, how red port loses its colour ageing in wood, whereas white port gains colour. Ancient tramlines for rolling pipes of port about maintain their rigidity in the lodge, whereas today's plastic pipes wind their way flexibly from one pipe to another.

Warre was founded in 1670 and right through from 1729 to 1912 there was always a member of the family based in Oporto. It has the fine distinction of being the oldest British house in the trade; only Köpke, founded by the son of the Consul General for the Hanseatic towns in Lisbon in 1838, can boast of being older. John Clark was the original owner of the company that was to become Warre & Co in 1729. The Warres were always in the forefront of Oporto society. William Warre married Elizabeth Whitehead, sister of the British Consul, John Whitehead: his great-nephew, born in 1784, became Lt. General Sir William Warre during the Peninsular War. His magnificent portrait still hangs over the staircase in the Factory House.

It was in 1905 that the first member of the Symington family, A. J. Symington, who had started his wine career with Graham, joined Warre. The Warres continued to administer the London end, but it was the Symingtons, sons and grandsons of A. J. Symington, who have expanded the production and shipping business dramatically in Oporto in recent years.

Real Vinicola

The descendant of the Marquês de Pombal's company formed in

1756 is the Real Companhia Vinicola do Norte de Portugal, known variously as Real Vinicola or the Companhia Velha. Taken over by the State again after the 1974 revolution, this enormous establishment has just been "disinterventação-ed" from the State.

The original company was started as a sovereign company which meant that only the monarch, then Dom José I, could intervene; the articles were jointly signed on August 31st, 1756 between the king and his prime minister, Pombal. During a recent visit I saw these original articles which the king, in rather complicated, spidery writing, has signed "Rey" (King). It is nice irony that the surname of the moving force of the company now is a Mr Silva Reis (Kings).

Age and tradition are heavily respected by the Portuguese. It is the company's intention to start a museum soon, which when completed will house a glittering array of rare documents, maps, letters and books. It should become the *de facto* port museum and a must for those interested in the historical perspective, not just from the British, but more from the Portuguese point of view.

The lodges of Real Vinicola are impressive, not for their tradition, but for their sheer operational size. There are 110,000 square metres of cellars, twenty stainless steel tanks, each capable of holding two thousand pipes, and six bottling lines.

Other firms

In addition to these mainstream port companies, there are a number of other companies or names which also form an integral part of the whole. Some companies have, inevitably, fallen by the wayside during the last three hundred years, but such is the stamina of most names that they still exist in one form or another. Some of these continue to supply large quantities of port in containers to the cheaper end of the European port market, whereas others maintain their long established reputation as secondary label port shippers. In alphabetical order they are:

Barros Almeida

One of the largest Portuguese houses. The group's subsidiary companies include the Douro Wine Shippers' Association.

Borges & Irmão

As well known for their table wines as their ports, Borges are one of the older-established Portuguese companies.

J. W. Burmester

Small, but still independent, Burmester was founded in 1730 by two partners, John Nash, an Englishman, and Heinz Burmester, a German. The partnership was dissolved in 1789 but Burmester continued on his own.

Butler, Nephew

Founded in 1789 by John Nash, fresh from breaking away from Burmester and his clerk, James Butler. The "Nephew" stands for James Butler's nephew, Robert, who joined in 1809. The firm is now owned by Gonzalez Byass.

Cruz

The largest-selling brand of port in France, which is the leading port-consuming market, Cruz has no history as a company in Portugal. The port behind the Cruz label is supplied by several different companies, mainly Messias. Formed in the mid 1970s, the company has one of the most modern bottling lines in the Entreposto and, since 1978, all Porto Cruz is bottled here.

Feuerheerd

Founded in 1815 by the twenty-two-year-old Diedrich Feuerheerd from Hamburg, as a general merchant company. His son, Hermann Feuerheerd, became sole owner in 1881 and transformed the company into being a respected port shipper. Their famous and much loved Quinta la Rosa remained in the family, but the firm is now owned by Barros Almeida.

Gonzalez Byass

This great sherry house decided to branch into the port trade in 1896. They shipped their vintage ports under the Quinta Roriz label at the beginning of the century under an arrangement with the Van Zeller family.

Hunt Roope

Its origins centre around the old West of England families of Newman, Roope, Holdworth, Hunt and Teage. Founded in 1735, the most famous partner was Cabel Roope who bought the lovely Eirha Vela quinta for the company. The quinta is now run by the Newman family in association with Cockburns, and the business since 1956 has been run by Ferreira.

C. N. Kopke

The oldest port shipper of them all. Founded in 1638 by Christiano Kopke, this company is now owned by Barros Almeida. The German Kopkes intermarried with the Dutch Van Zellers and shipped the wines of the excellent Quinta Roriz during the nineteenth century, before they were handled by Gonzalez Byass.

Martinez Gassiot

This was founded in 1797 in London, by a Spaniard, Sebastian Gonzalez Martinez, who was joined by Peter Gassiot in 1822. The firm acquired their first lodge in Vila Nova de Gaia in 1834. Martinez always favoured bulk shipments, rather than using their own name. In 1961 they were bought by John Harvey, thus joining their one-time keen rival, Cockburn.

Morgan

Morgan Brothers was founded in 1715 by a Mr Haughton from Clerkenwell, London. Aaron Morgan joined the firm at the turn of the century. One of Morgan's brands, "Dixon's Double Diamond", has an assured place in history as it was mentioned by Dickens in *Nicholas Nickleby* – "A magnum of the Double Diamond, David; to drink the health of Mr Linkinwater". In 1952 Morgan was bought by Croft and so is now owned by International Distillers and Vintners.

Poças

Established in 1918, Poças Junior is one of the newest, but one of the most progressive and chauvinistic Portuguese port shippers. All their ports are bottled in Vila Nova de Gaia and one of their specialities is that when sending vintage ports to the U.S.A. they always decant the wine first and then ship.

Robertson

Robertson Brothers became the successors to the old firm of Rebello Valente in 1881. They kept the name Rebello Valente for their vintage ports including the legendary 1931. One popular partner, James Robertson Rodger, was killed in an accident playing polo in London in 1925. Robertson is now owned by Sandeman.

Silva & Cosens

A Portuguese, Bruno da Silva, started importing his country's wines into England. One of his sons founded Silva & Cosens in Portugal in 1862 and merged with Dow in 1887. Dow's port is therefore shipped by Silva & Cosens which is one of the Symington's main companies.

Smith Woodhouse

Founded in 1784 by Christopher Smith from Cheapside, London, the firm's name became Smith Woodhouse in 1828 after William Woodhouse joined him in 1810. Famed for some excellent vintage port years in the later nineteenth century, the company now belongs to the Symington family.

VII
Oporto

THERE IS A saying "Lisbon plays, Coimbra studies, Braga prays and Porto works". Oporto is Portugal's second city and very much the capital of the north. Textiles have now taken over from wine as the dominant industry, yet there are certain places so entangled with the port trade that they should be on every serious visitor's list of things to see. To understand these bastions of tradition, elegance and, at times, sheer Britishness, it helps to know the city slightly.

Oporto was an important centre when Lisbon was still under the Moors. The people refer to their city as "the cradle of liberty" since the time when, in the thirteenth century, the Oporto burghers defied the ruling bishop. In the age of discovery, vast quantities of treasure came into the city. By 1500 Vasco da Gama had voyaged to India and the East and Pedro Alvares Cabral had brought back gold, sugar and spices from Brazil, thus making Portugal's King Manuel II the richest king in Europe. In the nineteenth century Oporto witnessed many revolutions against authority. Today it is a businessman's city and remains justly proud of its past – the rivalry between Oporto and Lisbon runs deep.

Oporto is still finding it difficult to steer itself into the twentieth century, let alone prepare itself for the twenty-first. Little has changed in the last one hundred and fifty years. Strong granite houses with terracotta roofs are interspersed by electric trams that never seem to go out of service. Many churches and towers add a baroque look. This style was initiated by an Italian, Niccolo Nazzoni, who invaded Oporto with his architecture in the early eighteenth century; his finest work may still be seen in the Sé (Cathedral), which was a fortress church in the twelfth century, and also in the Igreja dos

Clérigos, where there is a marvellous panoramic view from the top of the tower. Other places to visit are the Igreja São Francisco, where the interior is a triumph of baroque richness, Igreja Santa Clara, with its beautiful gilded woodwork and magnificent silver on the altars, and the Pálacio da Bolsa (Stock Exchange), with its splendid Arabian Hall. Portugal enriched itself from the New World and its merchant venturers brought back quantities of treasure. Even a half day spent exploring with a guide book – and perhaps a co-operative taxi, for the steep, often cobbled streets are tiring – will reward you.

The thing I most enjoy about Oporto's architecture is the use of the blue and white tiles, known as *azulejos*. They are delightfully exhibited in the main railway station (Estacão de São Bento), where the high walls of the spacious entrance lobby are covered with scenes of everyday life in modern Portugal – or modern as it was when these were painted and arranged by Jorge Colaço in 1930. Historic events, such as the entry of King João I into Oporto and his capture of Ceuta in 1415 are also recorded.

These *azulejos* are found all over Portugal, but I believe they are best when depicting vineyard scenes. In the main square of Viseu, the capital of the Dão table wine region south of the Douro Valley, there is a massive mural of *azulejos* and in the bustling railway station at Pinhão, in the middle of the port producing area, there are evocative individual vineyard scenes that show activities easily recognizable today. One of the nastier visual effects of the 1974 Revolution was that posters and spray-gun slogans covered many of these beautiful sights, as well as spattering the walls of most historic buildings. Fortunately, most of them have now been cleaned up and restored.

During the day, the centre of Oporto is noisy and not very clean. At night, it is reminiscent of the neon light era of the early 1930s. Traffic hurrying through the narrow streets is disorganized and many shops have no window displays, preferring to beckon you inside before you know what they are selling. The streets are full of ancient motor machinery, the pavements of swarthy moustachioed youths. The Portuguese require a great deal of knowing. They do not open their hearts to the visitor straight away. When they do, they are amongst the most friendly and helpful people in the world and their friendship, once established, is much valued.

The Factory House

This is the name of the headquarters of the British "factors" or merchants who, between them, formed the British "Factory", an association somewhat similar to a medieval guild. There were "Factories" in both Oporto and Lisbon. The British Factory only used the present house from when it was built in 1790 to 1807. Since 1814, the Factory House has been the headquarters of the British Association, composed of British port wine shippers, plus their partners and individual directors as members. At present there are twelve member firms.

The Factory House is in the Rua do Infante Dom Henrique, which, because of the congregations of British merchants there, was formerly known as the Rua Nova dos Ingleses, where the British merchants used to gather to discuss their business, often in the street itself. The delightful painting of this, by J. J. Forrester, done in 1834, is now the property of Offley Forrester (see page 14). There are crowds of upright gentlemen, in frock coats and top hats, in animated groups; some of them can be identified from family portraits of the period.

The Factory House is the imposing granite building to the left before you enter the tunnel that takes you from Oporto across the double decker bridge to Vila Nova de Gaia. It is, without doubt, the most British of all British institutions. Although it is not open and casual visitors cannot be shown round, it is well worthwhile seeking an introduction in advance to one of the firms who may be able to arrange with the treasurer for you to see it, as it may be considered as possibly the most important single thing to see in Oporto as far as the port lover is concerned.

The cost of building this elegant Georgian mansion came from a special contribution fund that Consul Whitehead levied on all goods exported from the city in British ships; the Factory House was to be used as an office for the Consul, as a place for public meetings to elect various Factory officials, to give receptions to visiting dignitaries and as a club for the members of the Factory House.

The building of such a mansion by the British in the middle of Oporto indicates the sense of permanence enjoyed by the British port shippers towards the end of the eighteenth century; although the British Empire has diminished since that day, the rigid splendours of the Factory still exist and flourish. For the past hundred and fifty years it has been the headquarters of the British Association, membership of which, confined to twelve British port companies, now consists of: Cockburn Smithes, Croft, Delaforce, Graham, Guimarãens, Martinez Gassiot, Offley Forrester, Robertson Brothers, Sandeman, Silva & Cosens, Taylor Fladgate & Yeatman, and Warre. These twelve companies, through comparatively recent takeovers, have now subdivided into five groups; although each company retains its individual voting powers, it is effectively the five British companies (Cockburn, Croft, Sandeman, Silva & Cosens and Taylor) who keep the Factory House financially alive.

The treasurer of the British Association is elected on a rota basis for an annual term, during which he has complete autonomy and responsibility for the Factory House. However, such is the established friendship between all these companies that it is a credit to those involved that the spirit and tradition of this remarkable self-perpetuating club remain not only unaltered but also extremely healthy.

The stark grey granite blocks from which the House is built ensure an even temperature throughout the year. The spacious entrance hall is thus always chilly – but gives the visitor an idea of what such a house was like before central heating. The massive unsupported granite staircase leads past royal and noble portraits. No outside city noises can be heard.

The rooms are each a magnificent slice of history: in one, the walls are lined with sets of priceless Spode and Davenport china, another is hung with nineteenth century maps; *The Times* newspaper is always displayed in a glass cabinet beside a copy exactly a hundred years old. A huge ballroom with dazzling chandeliers that light up to look like diamonds and a graceful balcony awaits the next grand occasion. For the tercentenary ball of Croft, in 1978, the staircase was wreathed up its length with all the wild flowers of the Douro, donated and arranged by rival port shippers' wives. The ballroom thronged with long dresses being swirled around the creaking floor by elegant dinner-jacketed guests, and the band played on and on.

The visitors' books go back to 1812 and the signatures of Wellington's staff, who were entertained at the Factory, can still be seen. The library contains more than twenty thousand volumes. I know of no other building that is so forbidding when it is empty, yet so full of life when people are enjoying themselves there; it is as though the Factory House is like a clock that stops when the last person leaves and can only be wound up with the advent of more people.

There is a luncheon every Wednesday for those port-shippers who are members and their guests – men only. It is a ritual, a tradition. Dry white port or sherry is served as an aperitif. The assembled company, which usually numbers about thirty, then files into the dining-room. Each contingent orders his own table wine, the main course is one to which you help yourself. The food now is simple but excellent. All the wines and ports are decanted and sit waiting on the white tablecloth. Two ports are always served: an old tawny port usually from the treasurer's own firm and a vintage port. Since 1856, it has been customary for all members, upon election, to present fourteen cases, equivalent to a quarter cask, of their firm's vintage port. There has been no inflation in this part of "forever England". A game which never loses its fun or excitement is always played: guess the year and shipper of the vintage port. Comments must be kept in perspective, because the port could be your own. Guests, who often include Portuguese bankers and lawyers, join in this happy ritual. You may see the British Consul talking to a distinguished port shipper who has now retired, alongside the managing director of another port shipper with his French agent, who is in animated conversation with a rival port shipper. The House thus still acts as a meeting place for the British shippers; it is a unique forum for wine merchants.

The Factory House really comes into its own, however, when a formal dinner is being held; although this cannot always be on the scale of the 1911 centenary dinner celebrating the restoration of the Factory by the British Army to the eleven factors during the Peninsular War. Then, on the eleventh day of the eleventh month at eleven o'clock in the evening, eleven descendants of the first eleven members gathered for a feast of eleven courses, with eleven wines: the menu included "lamprey sucking pig and caviarre", the wines included "1897 Hock, selected Riesling grape, Borges 1820 vintage port and Douro Brandy 1815".

The remarkable thing about the dining-room is that there are actually two rooms, both of identical size and each capable of seating forty-six persons. Two sets of folding doors lead from one room to the other. In the first room, where the Wednesday luncheons are held, members and their guests sit at a long, rounded mahogany table, with graceful chandeliers (now electrically powered) overhead. The second dining-room is where everyone moves to enjoy the vintage port; by tradition, just before this exodus takes place, you are served with a glass – only one – of delicious very old tawny port, always decanted, which is irreverently referred to as "mouthwash". The next moment everyone rises, napkins clutched in their hands, and all move through the doors to sit down in the adjoining room in exactly the same order as before, but here candles provide the only light, flickering on the lavish bowls of fruit and walnuts and reflected in the laden decanters. Now the vintage port can be enjoyed to the full without any aroma of food hanging in the air. Toasts are always proposed to "The Queen" and "The President of the Republic".

Other famous institutions

The Oporto Cricket and Lawn Tennis Club

Although this is a true club in that it is not open to non-members, except for members' guests, it is so much a place where traditions of virtually pre-1939 life are preserved that anyone who is likely to come to Oporto may be interested in knowing of its existence. Situated on the Rua Campo Alegre, it is usually referred to by the British as the "British Club" and by the Portuguese as the "Club Inglês". It is the focal point of English-speaking people and is the result of the 1967 merging of the Oporto British Club, which was founded in 1904, and the Cricket Club. The Cricket Club was founded in 1855 and moved to the present site in 1860.

Cricket matches typify the Englishness of this club: four or five matches are played each summer against "foreign" touring teams, which may be the MCC, the Eton Ramblers, or a team made up of members of the British wine trade, all of whom descend on Oporto with obvious relish. Cucumber sandwiches are served at tea-time, Pimm's cups in the early evening. It is all very delightful, very "British Oporto". There is a swimming-pool, a cricket field which doubles as a soccer pitch, a squash court and four lawn tennis courts, a billiard table and one for ping-pong (not here called "table tennis"). A handful of bedrooms, a bar and excellent dining-room are all tended by local club servants who never seem to grow older or speak English any better.

The Club Portuense

Ironically, this, the Portuguese Club, in Rua Candido dos Reis, is far more like a club in London's St James's than the British Club, whose activities are primarily sporting. The splendid building of the Club Portuense has high eighteenth-century rooms and an imposing staircase, the atmosphere is quiet and the staff move around with dignity; everything evokes a way of life that moves placidly according to conventions. This, being a club, is not open to visitors.

Instituto do Vinho do Porto

The third attraction in Oporto directly linked to the wine trade is the fount of all – the handsome Georgian building which used to house a bank and is now the Instituto do Vinho do Porto, or the Port Wine Institute. It is barely a hundred yards from the Factory House and again, if the serious student of wine is able to arrange to see inside by a request to someone in the port trade, a brief visit will be worthwhile.

Founded in 1933, the Instituto do Vinho do Porto rigorously defends its all-embracing rôle of controlling the port industry; it sees its function as one giving a state guarantee to a product that has been made by private enterprise. The Instituto's activities include the formation of overall policy, research, publicity, the maintenance of quality through blind tastings of wines, and a check on all movement of every port; from the time when it enters a lodge the record of its movement is strictly kept.

Inside the almost forbidding facade, a wide granite staircase leads to a mezzanine landing, where you can see a stone, three feet high, which originally marked the 1756 boundary of the port wine region. The rooms include beautiful reception salons, decorated in Wedgwood green with an amusing ceiling painting of Bacchus in one of them; there are also numerous impersonal stores of records and files, plus lab-type rooms full of busy men in white coats, usually gazing at huge graphs or else observing test-tubes of bubbling liquid. The Instituto's seal, which you will see as a paper strip over the top of every bottle of port, is awarded only as the result of all this serious consideration – quality is firmly the name of the game.

Solar do Vinho do Porto

A month after the Revolution in April 1974, the Director of the Instituto do Vinho do Porto, Eng. João Brito e Cunha, opened the Solar do Vinho do Porto. It is situated in the cellars of the Museu Romántico at the Quinta da Macieninha, which is near the Palácio de Cristal. This delightful, elegant property was built by one of Oporto's leading merchants, António Ferreira Pinto Basto, in the early nineteenth century; it faces the River Douro and is surrounded by spacious, well-tended grounds.

As this port showplace was created expressly to publicize port to the visitor, it is open most days, although it is advisable to check about this beforehand.

An enormous selection of ruby, tawny, dated and vintage ports are on display at the Solar and it is therefore an ideal ambiance in which to taste as wide a selection as possible. No entrance charge is made and, depending on its age, a glass of port will cost anything between Esc. 50 and Esc. 250. Many ports found here are only exported in limited quantities, so it is an ideal place to pioneer knowledge of wines you may never see anywhere else.

Above the Solar is a museum housing the personal effects and furniture of the exiled King Charles of Sardinia who died in 1894, so the Solar is of interest to members of accompanying families who may not wish to taste but who will enjoy seeing the house and its gardens.

VIII
Vintage Port

FEW TYPES OF wine produce more excitement, bluff and downright enjoyment than vintage port. These two words are evocative of banquets, loyal toasts and great occasions; state dinners and regimental messes would not be the same without vintage port, universities would be deprived of one of their pillars of postprandial discussion. Vintage port is an essential ingredient for the maintenance of the quality of life.

"The first wine which could worthily claim the title of vintage port" was conceived during the 1775 vintage. One year before the American War of Independence . . . this happily coincided, perhaps on a chicken and egg basis, with the evolvement of the elongated bottle which had a short neck, and for the first time, a sufficiently long body for the bottle to be binned on its side, thus enabling the wine to stay in contact with the cork. André Simon in *Bottle-screw Days* (1926) puts the date of the final development of the port bottle as we recognize it today as being 1784.

The vintage port of that era was almost certainly a very big, fat, robust red port that was bottled when it was three to four years old. It was then binned and left to mature in bottle until such time as it was considered to be at its peak for drinking. The basic change in the past two hundred years is that now it is mandatory for vintage port to be bottled when it is two years old, or in other words when the rich and deep ruby wine is at its early peak, untainted by any tawny flavour resulting from cask maturation. Otherwise, the same principles apply.

The concept of vintage port is simple, yet the complexities of taste are immense. The achievement of a great vintage port is rare; once perfected the enjoyment is intense. During a year when all the elements have enabled the grapes to be harvested in absolutely prime condition, the port shipper will think to himself "maybe this could be a vintage year". It is not often that God looks so propitiously and frequently on the Douro Valley; maybe not for five years, as between 1970 and 1975, but sometimes in two years together, as in 1934 and 1935. God does not like averages, but for the statistician it seems that the elements vitally coincide about three times a decade.

Experience has shown the port shipper that it is necessary to wait two winters and a summer before a final judgement can be made as to whether "he has a vintage on his hands", because the young port can change in character during this perod. Seasonal temperature variations do cause the young wine to oscillate in well-being; after the second winter the little chap has settled down. Sandeman's, in fact, bottled their 1944 port as a vintage but, after the superb vintages of 1945 and 1947, they felt that this was not showing sufficiently well to carry their vintage name, and so they disgorged the whole bottling and put it into their blends. This shows the responsibility a shipper feels towards the name of his house.

Each shipper has his own style or character. This is derived from two factors: first, the geographical location of the vineyards within the Cima Corgo, second, the tasting skills of those who care for the wines in Gaia, handed down from generation to generation, that are needed to create a perfectly balanced port. Most shippers own one prime estate which forms the basis for their vintage ports. Even though vintage port represents at most only two per cent of annual port exports in a prolific year, these vineyards alone cannot produce each shipper's requirements, so it is necessary to complement the style of wine produced with that of another vineyard or vineyards to balance maturity with grip; fullness with fragrance. These other vineyards have usually been supplying Shipper X or Y for many decades, sometimes for centuries, and the friendship between farmer and shipper in such cases is often so lasting that these vineyards may be considered an annex to the shippers' own quinta.

A classic example of how different shippers provide different styles is that Taylor's Quinta da Vargellas is close to the Spanish frontier, where the soil gets progressively harder and vines often produce enormously deep, full-bodied wine. Croft's Quinta da Roêda, near Pinhão, is a flatter vineyard, producing fragrant, lighter wine, Quinta do Noval's elegant higher vineyards produce a wine that in depth is somewhere between the two, yet is distinctly different. The second factor which differentiates one shipper's vintage port from another is exactly how each shipper selects, blends, treats and matures his port. But each jealously guards his own method.

During the two winters and one summer (from, say, October 1977 to March 1979) the shipper is constantly tasting and blending (and praying). If all has gone well, the buzz will be soon felt in London as in Oporto: first, casual asides may reverberate around the Wednesday luncheons at the Factory House (see page 103) "How are your 1977's looking?" Then much chattering about prices. During this time, each shipper who is thinking of declaring a vintage submits samples to the IVP authorities (see page 105). At the same time, he must state the total quantity that he wishes to bottle. Once this is approved, it is entirely up to the shipper as to whether he will "declare" or not; assuming that he wants to, he will then offer his vintage port to his customers.

This entails sending a quantity of quarter or half bottle samples to each shipper's agent in the UK. The agent in turn will then send these out to his major customers to try and persuade them to buy his vintage rather than that of someone else. Comparative blind tastings are held up and down the country and there gradually evolves a kind of trade feeling that certain shippers' vintages are more outstanding than others. The buyer will then select a number of shippers that he believes have made the best vintage of that year, and then buy at opening prices.

As vintage ports are not declared each year, it may well be five or more years (as between 1970 and 1975) since the buyer has tasted similar young vintage ports and, as tasting is so much a function of memory and association, the buyer may well have to start re-educating himself each time a vintage port tasting is held. Also the very nature of the wine is such that what smells and tastes magnificent now may well peak too early and not mature into the classic mould that is intended. It is vital when tasting young vintage ports to be constantly alert, so as to envisage the taster's objective – to gauge how each wine is going to smell and taste when it is fully mature.

The first blind tasting of vintage ports that I went to was with that fine buyer and colleague, Don Lovell, Master of Wine. We were to taste the 1960s. Most of these had been produced in the traditional lagar (or treading) method, as the autovinification vats had not yet been wholly accepted by the port shippers at that time. I was astounded when I saw the depth, the robustness, the concentration of colour in the row of tasting glasses each containing an equal sample, arranged on a perfect white cloth like soldiers – the sheer matted complexities of taste and velvet strength of these two-year-old ports were a marvel to experience. I then adopted the adage that the more vulgar the young vintage port is, the more sensational and good looking it will emerge in its prime – it will give more fun and depth of feeling to the drinker.

People often ask why more vintage port cannot be produced. It is quite simple. 80 per cent of all port exported is ruby or tawny port, aged in wooden casks, bottled and then sold. There is only a limited amount of quality port in the Douro Valley so, if the very best of this port were always reserved for vintage port, then these ruby and tawny ports would be deprived of the corresponding quantity of wine to keep up their quality during each year that a vintage were declared. Equally, it is an unwritten law that no port shipper ever publicises the total amount of vintage port that he makes during a vintage year. Different shippers have different policies as to how much they can or should make. It is likely that about 250,000 cases of vintage port (2.4 million bottles) are made during great vintage years, leaving about six million cases (72 million bottles) to be made into tawny and ruby ports. Quantity is thus always limited. There may come a day when port shippers adopt the Château Mouton Rothschild principle of stating on the label exactly how much was produced by that port house in that particular year, but this has not yet happened.

Furthermore, it is the tawny and ruby ports which have universal appeal and most international potential. Vintage ports have a limited, albeit vital, part to play in the total port picture.

It is an accepted rule of thumb that the port shipper chooses his blends for his vintage port on the basis that they will peak or mature in about ten to fifteen years. The wine will have had two years maturing in cask, breathing through wood.

Harvesting: the grapes are loaded for transportation.

Harvesting: the grapes are brought to the wine centre.

Vila Nova de Gaia: a vintage port cellar.

Vila Nova de Gaia: interior of port wine lodge showing pipes.

Vila Nova de Gaia: interior of port wine lodge showing blending vats.

An historical scene: the pipes of port are being offloaded in Vila Nova de Gaia after their three-day journey from the Douro Valley.

Entreposto of Vila Nova de Gaia at the mouth of the Douro River.

Oporto, looking westwards to the Atlantic, with Vila Nova de
Gaia in the background.

Port shippers' signs along the waterfront in Vila Nova de Gaia
indicate the proximity of their lodges.

Barcos rabelos no longer transport the wine; but they are moored
along the waterfront in Vila Nova de Gaia and used for
promotional purposes.

Two celebrations, half a century apart, of the reopening of the
Factory House on 11 November 1811 after the evacuation of
Portugal by the French army. Traditionally, celebrations are held
on 11 November at 11 o'clock by representatives of the original
eleven families in the British Association.

Bottling

All vintage port is now bottled in Vila Nova de Gaia, and, to my mind, a lot of fuss has been made in recent years about whether vintage port should be bottled in Portugal or in the U.K. Vintage port has never been bottled in quantity anywhere else. Except during World War II, when the 1942 and 1945's were necessarily bottled in Portugal, it was the custom and tradition for major buyers in the U.K. – such as many large concerns and historic wine merchants – to bottle the vintage port that they had each bought from the shippers; the argument was that they could do it better. However, as vintage port is such a boisterous strong wine when it is being bottled, from a technical point of view, it can be bottled without losing any of its fine characteristics by even the most junior woman on the least fast bottling line. The controversy – Oporto versus British bottling – as reflected in seemingly endless letters in the trade press, was decided when, in 1974, the IVP determined that in future all vintage port would be bottled at source, that is, in Vila Nova de Gaia. So the 1975 became the first vintage port to be exclusively bottled in the country of its origin.

This, I think, is a right decision, if only because I once saw in a shop window in Denmark a well-known shipper's vintage port, bottled in a Burgundy bottle with a rather garish "punk" type capsule standing upright. What might the wine have been like inside such a bottle (which would anyway have been awkward to decant off its crust)? Other countries than the United Kingdom do drink vintage port and so the necessary controls have been applied to safeguard the image of what is one of the world's most exclusively traditional drinks.

Once bottled, the port will mature much more slowly than wines of similar age that are maturing in wood. Thus although theoretically the 1977s should be ready to be enjoyed in two plus twelve years, bringing us to 1992 in practice, such a vintage is likely to have a much longer potential life.

Decanting

"When shall I drink it?" This is perhaps the most familiar cry of the port man. Let us go back to the young, immature, bursting-with-energy vintage ports when they are first exposed to the outside world. Wine is a living organism; the similarities between a vintage port's life cycle and our own are uncanny. It is as difficult to look at a child and say that he or she will reach their prime at a certain age as it is to predict the length of time that a vintage port will take to mature. Some men mature early, some never grow up; some are ambitious, others less so. Some women develop at an early stage, some become fat and lazy, some remain young, others age gracefully. It is the same with port. To say that a man or woman will be at his or her prime at an exact moment is no easy task – equally with port. Tastes vary; some people enjoy youth, others prefer age, so not everyone will enjoy drinking a vintage port at the same stage of maturity.

The important thing to remember is that there is no "right" or "wrong" time to open that bottle of 1963 or 1970, for you can never really leave a vintage port until it is too old. If you think that the bottle you have in your cellar may be getting past its prime, think of your grandfather or great-aunt: treat it, like them, with a little bit of extra care. Be kind and understanding. Do not expect it to be vigorous. Let it breathe. Taste it immediately after you have decanted it and see how much life is still in the wine. It is a marvellous experience communing with the aged – they always have something worthwhile to give before they finally fade away.

The classic advice of when to decant is the older the port, the nearer the meal. The timing also depends on whether a fuller, tighter taste – just decanted – is preferred, or whether a softer, more relaxed approach – decanted some hours beforehand – is required. Unless the vintage port is 1945 or earlier, my advice is to decant double the time you first thought of. Four hours' breathing space is minimal.

All vintage port needs decanting because during its life lying on its side, a crust or deposit will form along the bottom of the bottle. It is for this reason that a white line or dot is usually painted on the base of the bottle at the time of bottling so that whenever the bottle is moved you can always put it back the right way up (with the line on top), so that the crust always forms in the same area. When the time comes to open a bottle of vintage port, it is best to leave it standing upright for twenty-four hours, to let the soft crust or deposit fall to the bottom.

Most vintage ports have wax seals and a very long cork with the shipper's name and date printed on it. So if the label has come off, do not worry – the cork will reveal all. Use a knife to crack off the wax seal, gently tapping so that the wax falls clear of the bottle. Wipe the now exposed cork with a clean napkin. Take your longest corkscrew to pull out the cork. Insert this steadily and gently, working it down to the base of the cork but try not to pierce this, as little bits of cork may then fall into the wine. Pull the cork without jerking the bottle – steadily. When the cork comes out, wipe the inside of the bottle neck again with the napkin.

If you have a silver hook-nosed wine filter or funnel with tiny holes in it, put this into the neck of your glass decanter and pour the vintage port slowly into it. If you do not have such a filter, clean muslin is fine to use, but not if it is tainted with anything that smells. Pour slowly, gradually tilting the bottle and stop as soon as you notice even a trace of crust or deposit appearing in the neck of the bottle; because the glass of the port bottle is dark, it helps to have a candle or some bright light underneath the neck. A trick here is to decant the port into a glass jug first. The open neck makes it easier to pour into through muslin rather than the narrow neck of the decanter, then pour slowly into the decanter itself. We drink first with our eyes; a clear glass of wine is more appetising than a cloudy one, even though the taste can be the same, so do not attempt to empty the whole bottle into the decanter, leave an inch or two at the bottom of the bottle. It is quality not quantity that counts here.

You will rarely find vintage port served at luncheons in shippers' lodges in Vila Nova de Gaia – nor at their quintas in the Douro Valley. The reason is not just one of scarcity or expense, nor really that, as many will say, vintage port does not taste at its best in the Portuguese climate. It is that, having selected the original blends for the vintage port, the port shipper has no further control over it, the job is done. Whereas old tawny ports are a judicious blend of the taster's arts and skills, he is being an "éleveur" to the wine, caring for its foibles, keeping it clean by constantly racking it, taking enormous pleasure in seeing it mature, deciding whether it can go on to be a thirty-year old tawny or be at its prime as a ten-year old tawny, or evolve into a robust full ruby or vintage character. In essence, whilst a vintage port reflects the traditional style of the port shipper, an old tawny port reflects the particular skills of the port shipper.

Official descriptions of aged port

Vintage Port

Vintage port must state clearly on the bottle's label the year that it was produced, for example, 1980. It must also state the year in which it was bottled, for example, bottled in 1982. The date on the label refers solely to true vintage port and it is only vintage port that need be bought, whether by universities, clubs, messes or individuals so as to be "laid down". You lay down a bottle or case of vintage port in order to mature the wine. The sooner you buy it, ideally at opening prices, the less expensive it should be but these days the price of producing port tends to rise each year, so an early purchase is a good investment, whether you are laying down for eventual drinking or with some idea of later selling and reinvesting.

The vintage port market traditionally has been dominated by the British port shippers, Cockburn, Croft, Delaforce, Dow, Fonseca, Graham, Martinez, Sandeman, Taylor, Warre being the best known. Two Portuguese port shippers who must be included in this list are Ferreira and Noval, are also well-known.

Other Portuguese port shippers were effectively shut out of the U.K. vintage port market and, during the nineteenth and early twentieth centuries, it was only vintage ports that carried the name of their shippers. They were, in essence, branded ports.

All other port was sold to wine merchants and breweries and bore their name on the labels, not that of the port shippers. So the only recurring port names that anyone ever heard were those of the shippers of vintage port. In the meantime, Portuguese port shippers were getting established and selling large quantities of port, not vintage port, to Europe, notably in France, in South America, notably Brazil, and Africa, especially Angola. As each company established its own style and market, there was a demand for finer quality ports. But because only the British understood the niceties of vintage port, it was incumbent on the Portuguese shippers to develop other ways of describing quality and age for their better ports and thus were born "dated ports".

Dated Ports

These are like chalk is to cheese as compared with vintage ports, as they are not allowed to be bottled until they have matured in wooden casks for seven years. They are thus tawny ports, having lost their ruby colour whilst slumbering in wooden vats or casks, but they are tawny ports made from the wines of one year as distinct from being a blend of years. Legally, they now also have to have the year in which they were bottled stated on the label. So a bottle stating 1964, bottled in 1972, is in effect an eight-year-old tawny port, ready for drinking now. It will not improve in bottle, whereas of course a 1963 bottled in 1965 is a true vintage port and will certainly improve in bottle. These dated ports are mainly found in the USA and Continental Europe.

Late Bottled Vintage

The other two ways of expressing an aged port are "late bottled vintage" and "port with indication of age". Again, these two descriptions produce quite different styles.

Late bottled vintage, or LBV, is a sound, full port, produced in non-vintage years, such as 1961, bottled after maturing in wooden casks for four to six years. This style was originally designed to produce a vintage style or vintage character port, that would have the richness of a vintage port but would not be so expensive. By being allowed to bottle the port with a two-year tolerance, different levels of maturing are achieved and as a concept it is losing favour amongst most port shippers, but not amongst port drinkers.

Crusting Port

Its even less defined predecessor "crusting port" was omitted from the Instituto do Vinho do Porto's new regulations governing age, which came into force in July 1974. Crusting port was a blend of two or three years of first class wines, which had matured in wooden casks for three or four years before being bottled. They threw a light deposit or crust after some years in bottle, hence their name.

Indication of Age Ports

Ports with an indication of age are true tawny ports in that they have matured for ten, twenty, thirty or over forty years in wooden casks before they are bottled. All natural deposit having fallen out of them, they are marvellous, clean silky wines. Over the years, by constant surveillance and racking, the shippers have done the decanting for you and, as one port shipper remarked with a twinkle in his eye "Better to let the tannic deposit stay in the cask rather than allow it into your stomach."

The indicated age is not an absolute figure. It is the average age of the wines in that blend. So a port which states "Aged for 10 years in wood", comprises blends that could be six years old and fourteen years old.

Passing the Port

H. M. Bateman sums it all up in his 1924 cartoon "The man who passed the port the wrong way". There is only one greater faux pas, and that is not to pass the port around the table at all.

At formal dinner parties, the port decanter is left on the table at the end of dinner in a silver coaster. The host traditionally fills his guest's glass immediately to his right, then his own and passes the decanter to his left. Each fills his own glass about two thirds full until the decanter is returned to the host. Cigars are only lit once everyone has tasted the port, otherwise the smoke will detract from that initial enjoyment.

There are many explanations for this ritual. The crudest is that as most people are right handed it is easier to lift the decanter with the right hand pass it across the body to the left. It is also natural that the decanter should go clockwise. Both these are simple, yet logical. Another theory is that the ancient Celts held that all circular motions should be deiseal, or the right-hand turn. This was the lucky turn; the left-hand turn was illomened.

When the port decanter has gone round the table several turns, it is quite likely that animated conversation will result in a guest not noticing that the decanter is by his right side. It is considered bad manners and greedy to actually ask a fellow diner to pass the port. The convivial Dr Wright of Norwich in the 1850s was such a bottle stopper, and as the following exchange shows, has kindly given his name to the time immemorial password "Do you know Dr Wright of Norwich?"

In New York several years ago, I was at a Wine party – all there were Englishmen. The bottles were at my left hand, when a

Cumberland gentleman in a loud voice, asked me if I knew Dr. Wright of Norwich? I said innocently, and as a fact, "Yes, I knew a Dr. Wright of Norwich and that he stood high in his profession". This created a laugh and I found the phrase was intended to intimate that I was a bottle stopper! It seemed to be well known among my English friends and to have been used a lot by drinking men many years before I heard it. Pray, can any of your readers tell how it originated?

E. New York

Having known the late Dr. Wright of Norwich many years, I am enabled to say in answer to the query of E, that the Doctor was very convivial and also very apt to stop the bottle. Indeed so much so that the above phrase was common in the circles he frequented and he himself used to refer to its applicability to himself with perfect good humour.

J. P. O.
Notes & Queries 2nd Series,
Vol. *IX* – May 19th and June 16th 1860

When this innocent phrase floats across the dining room table, pause to check where the decanter is and, if on your right, pass it quickly to the empty glasses on your left. The Bishop of Norwich or Jones of the 60th will do quite adequately if Dr Wright's name escapes you.

Some hosts, to ensure this can never happen, invest in a port decanter with a rounded bottom that can only sit on the table in a specially constructed wooden frame. The frame stays in front of the host, so the decanter has always to return to him.

One of the most ingenious and charming constructions I have seen is "the railway", built around 1820 and designed after the Durham railway by Warden Shuttleworth. It is still used today on special occasions in the Senior Common Room of New College, Oxford. The railway is a board with tracks about six foot by eighteen inches and slopes from a height of two feet to ground level. Two containers on tiny wheels, one holding a bottle of hock, the other a decanter of port can be raised or lowered the full six feet by a pulley. Its purpose is to transport the port decanter across the fireplace without anyone getting up. Dons sit around small tables with their port and coffee after dinner. Ever since a rather jovial vicar kept getting up to pass the port across the fireplace and then tripped over, the railway has been used.

Outstanding years for vintage port

Waterloo, the great 1815 vintage port, was judged in Christie's Wine Review in 1973 to have lasted to the mid 1930s. The longevity of vintage ports is legendary. Several years towards the end of the nineteenth century, such as 1870, 1878 and 1896, produced superlative ports that are still lively today. In Christie's same review, the 1878 was reported, nearly a hundred years later, as "still holding well". Most port shippers still have the odd bottle of these great years secreted away in their lodges, but they are rarely seen in public.

Since 1900, there have been thirteen outstanding vintage port years. There have been many more declared vintage port years, but for one reason or another, these are exceptional. Any chance to drink even one small glass of these finest years should not be passed up.

Year	Number of shippers declared	Comments
1904	25	Classic quality; drying out now but still fine.
1908	26	A great vintage; holding well. Fuller than 1904. A rival to 1912. Cockburn, Croft and Taylor still showing well.
1912	25	Classic quality has ensured great reputation. Magnificent and full-bodied. Cockburn and Taylor still superb.
1927	30	Exceptional wines were made during this late vintage – started 3rd October. Grapes were ripe and picked in perfect hot conditions. Record number of shippers declared. Taylor an outstanding example.
1931	3	Excellent year after cool summer. Bumper quantities of the 1927 and the world economic conditions caused only three shippers to declare, thus its rarity value now. The legendary Noval and still fruity Rebello Valente typify this year.

Year	Number of shippers declared	Comments
1935	15	Similar in colour to the 1934s, but finer and more elegant. Cockburn, Croft, Sandeman and Taylor perfect now.
1945	22	Classic vintage rivalling 1912. Early vintage starting 10th September, but magnificent full-bodied character. Deep with great colour; a luscious bouquet and satisfying mouthful. Due to import licence restrictions in U.K. it was mostly bottled in Oporto.
1948	9	The 1948s can always be identified by their slightly burnt taste caused by the extremely hot summer which burnt many Cima Corgo grapes. Full-bodied, powerful and luscious. Graham, Fonseca and Taylor produced classic wines.
1955	26	High quality year; similar to 1935. Well-balanced, classic all-rounder wines. Tasting finely elegant now.
1960	24	Fine quality, plenty of colour and body. Vintage started early on September 12th as the weather then was extremely hot. Should have been an even greater vintage, but rain fell after September 24th. Still available in better restaurants.
1963	25	A classic vintage year both in quantity and quality. Picking took place in ideal conditions, hot days and cool nights. Full-bodied, fruity with great finesse. Will continue to develop. It is the vintage year now most favoured by restaurants. Croft regarded as a typical example.

Year	Number of shippers declared	Comments
1966	20	Elegant, fruity wines which are developing exceptionally well. The drought during the year produced high sugar contents which, matched with the welcome rain after September 26th, produced excellent quality, but limited quantity. Graham marvellous now. Scarce.
1977	22	The most recent generally declared vintage year, but outstanding in the depth, grip, fullness and elegance of its wines. Likely to last longer than either the 1970 (classic but soft) or the 1975 (fine and fruity).

In addition to the great 1960, 1963, 1966 and 1977 vintage ports, other years which are now generally available from wine merchants are 1967, 1970 and 1975. At the time of writing, the 1980s have just been declared by some shippers. I believe this is in many ways a watershed vintage. The wines are pleasingly correct with no outstanding virtues. Most shippers, with the major exception of Cockburns, have declared a shippers' vintage port. Croft and Delaforce have declared single quinta vintage ports – respectively Roêda and Corte. It is this latter trend – single estate wines – that I believe we shall see much more of in the next decades.

IX
Tasting

WINE TASTING CONJURES up different images to different people. To
the port shipper, it is an integral part of his daily life, practised
regularly in the Douro and Vila Nova de Gaia; to the wine merchant,
it is usually the deciding factor in choosing wines he can sell best; to
some, it seems marvellous that one can actually get paid for tasting
wine and to others, heart beats are missed under the awesome gaze of
the wine waiter poised to pour.

The main aim of tasting is to ensure that at all stages of the port's
life, those responsible are buying correctly; once bought, it makes the
bottle of port that much more enjoyable if you can taste it before
drinking it.

Tasting port is different from tasting wine. In the first place, there
are the complexities of the marriage between the wine and the
brandy; second, port is drunk after a certain degree of maturation so
the initial tasting has to bear in mind that a port is being selected on
its merits now for consumption in five, ten or twenty years. Nowhere
is this more true than with vintage port. At a blind vintage port
tasting, when you do not know which shippers' wine you are tasting,
you can have up to twenty different shippers' vintages. As vintage
port years tend to be every three years or so, most tasters have to
think back over a thousand days when they last tasted these
amazingly deep, fruity wines. Each sample is dark, matted, full and a
real mouthful. Buyers have to look ahead fifteen or twenty years to
decide which young vintage ports will last the course and mature to
classic satisfaction almost a generation later.

This is not the case when you are enjoying that vintage port or an
old tawny port a generation later, but the principles of port tasting

remain the same. Drinking a glass of port without tasting it is rather like eating with your eyes closed: you miss half the fun.

Stages of tasting

Always fill tasting glasses, preferably tulip shaped with a short stem, only one-third full. This will leave enough space for you to swill the port around in the glass giving it air in which to expand.

There are three basic elements that make up the art of tasting. The colour, the bouquet or nose and the actual taste. If all three are pleasing then the Douro farmer, the port shipper, and the wine merchant have not worked in vain. The colour should look bright – clear – giving an indication of what the port is going to taste like.

A ruby port should have a youthful, rich red appearance as befits its name. Tawny ports should have a mellower, more of a look of a sunset about them. White ports should have a yellowy straw-like hue. Vintage ports, if decanted properly, have a relaxed, mature look about them. The intense ruby colour should still be intact, but elegantly portrayed.

The bouquet or nose of the port being tasted is of fundamental importance. Most professional port tasters use their nose more than their mouth to gauge a port's quality. The bouquet or smell that you can get from nosing the wine adds a further dimension into the enjoyment of the taste. The consistency of the wine in the glass is all important. The beads or tears or "legs" of the wine that cling to the sides of the glass indicate quality and glycerine content. For example, they are more pronounced in an old tawny than in a younger tawny blended with red and white wines.

Now is the time to taste. To try and convey to someone else exactly what it is you taste in a wine is not easy. The sensation of tasting is a very personal and elusive thing. The actual sensations of taste are said to be: sweetness, bitterness and sourness. Somewhere between these parameters lies the taste that you experience.

The most important aspect of tasting is whether you like the port or not. It will say different things to different people. Try to identify the taste and position that taste in your memory. Always spit out the wine if there is a reliable receptacle nearby, as retention will spoil the next wine you taste. First impressions are usually right. It is "round and full", "fruity", "rich", "mellow"; when you have swallowed the wine and it runs down your throat, it has "depth", if it is smooth, it is "velvety". Do not be afraid to describe it in your own terminology. Write down your thoughts immediately. Everyone has their own code. "Dirty socks" and "straw bales" are two descriptions I have seen on a tasting sheet recently. Building up a mental library of wine tastes is not only immensely satisfying but fun as well.

Tasting in Portugal

The opportunity to taste port in Portugal, whether it is in a shipper's lodge in Vila Nova de Gaia or at a quinta in the Douro Valley, should not be missed. Tasting rooms in lodges are big, airy and spotlessly clean. Men and women in white coats go about their business with a very professional air. Human experience now blends with technological laboratory analyses. A most rewarding tasting is to have lined up on the white formica or marble bench a row of red ports in ascending age. By seeing one-, three-, five-, ten-, fifteen-, twenty-year-old ports side by side, the ageing process can really be appreciated and understood. The purplish-blue of the one-year-old gives way to ruby, then, through wood maturation, to a tawny colour and thence to a graceful old tawny colour.

In the Douro, a chance to taste the young ports during their first six months of life is an incredible experience. They are usually big and purple, yet fragrant and velvety – a marvellous, youthful blend of wild mountain tastes. Equally, at the other end of the scale, a glass of fifty-year-old or even older tawny port drunk from a cask that has remained in the same place in the same quinta for half a century is an unforgettable experience. The clean burnt beauty is the zenith of perfection.

Thus, remember that wherever you are, in a quinta in the Douro Valley, in a traditional tasting room in a port shipper's lodge, in a wine merchant's office or retail store, at a club wine tasting, in a restaurant or at home, much more can be gained from every glass if first you appreciate the colour, then the bouquet and finally the taste itself. Always be true to yourself and, bit by bit, a wealth of knowledge will be stored away. Confidence will suddenly take over from nervousness and you will happily find yourself voicing your comments to your friends.

Practicalities

As may be expected, there are several "don'ts" that are wise to heed. Do not talk whilst tasting. Nothing is more boring at a tasting than having someone keep exclaiming or muttering about the wines. It disturbs the concentration and interrupts the train of thought.

Make sure the glasses are clean. Do not put wine glasses in a dishwasher and then store them upside down in your glass cupboard. The trapped air often contaminates the inside of the glass and utterly spoils the wine. Do not use lipstick – especially if glasses are being shared at a tasting – lipstick on a glass ruins the taste.

Do not hold the bowl of the glass; always hold the stem or base. This is because the warmth of the hand can change the temperature of a wine substantially if held for some time.

Do not drink all the wine that is in the glass. At even a moderately serious tasting, spittoons or empty receptacles should be provided to spit into. Taste first, drink later.

Finally, beware of all the mumbo-jumbo that surrounds wine tasting. Within the overall guidelines set out here, you are free to make your own set of rules. (In the U.S.A. I have seen "tasting" described as a "terminal gustatory act".) Time and time again, people will tell you that you can gauge the quality of the port by how many "legs" it has; apparently, the more the better. Make up your own vocabulary: get stuck into "velvet", "dung", or "raspberries". Once an association is fixed in your memory bank, you will be able to summon it up the next time you taste that particular wine.

X
Gastronomy – Food and Wine

THROUGHOUT THE YEARS, each country has developed its own food
and wines, either according to what it can grow itself or what is easily
imported. Generations of eating and drinking achieve the generally
preferred natural combination. Certain styles of cooking and dishes
are known internationally because either their wines or other
beverages are known internationally; ex-patriates then start up
restaurants, employing people who speak the same language and
promote the food and wine of their own country. Harmony blends
with harmony.

Portuguese cuisine, to date, does not enjoy such an international
reputation. The Portuguese certainly travelled to the New World and
brought back rice and spices to enrich their food. They also explored
the Far East in the seventeenth century and there is a strong
Portuguese influence in certain parts of Africa and South America.
Today, most emigration is to France and thence to other European
countries, but the culinary habits they have taken with them tend
towards strong, virile peasant food rather than sophisticated special-
ity dishes.

Consequently, although there are many Portuguese waiters, there
are few Portuguese restaurants in Europe or North America. But
Portuguese gastronomy is a national delight and markedly different
from Spanish Latin Mediterranean cuisine because Portugal is an
Atlantic country.

Portuguese cooking is divided into seaboard and mountain areas,
and then subdivided into regional areas. In the former, up and down
Portugal's long coastline, lobster (*gosta*) and sardines (*sardinhas*)
prevail, with all the other tiny fish caught in the nets being

transformed into delicious fish soups (*sopa do mariscos*). In the mountain areas, bread is important and supplements rich pork dishes, smoked sausages, chicken and stews. *Presunto* (smoked ham), especially that from Chaves, is typically regional, as pigs wander almost wild in these desolate areas. Presunto with melon is a favourite dish. Olive oil is used liberally. Portugal's national dessert dish is the *pudim*, an egg custard with sauce.

Vegetables and fruit are found in abundance everywhere. But the unifying and thus national dish is the *bacalhau*, dried codfish. Bacalhau was originally produced to preserve cod by drying and salting it, so that it could be used on long sea voyages or for far destinations in the mountains. It became an important item in Anglo-Portuguese trading and, today, it is still the staple dish of Portugal. There are hundreds of ways of serving bacalhau, most based on mixing potatoes and a cheese sauce with the boiled cod. Wine, eggs and vegetables are added according to different recipes. For initiation into bacalhau, I suggest Bolinhos de Bacalhau, which are delightful golden fried puffs of cod mixed with egg yolks – extremely tasty.

Four courses are customary at meals in Portugal, whether in a restaurant or at home; soup to begin with, then fish, meat and a *pudim* or tart. Soup is almost mandatory, but does not suffer anything from being so. The *calde verde*, or green soup, found everywhere in the north, is delicious. It is made from huge dark green cabbage leaves, very finely cut or shredded, and potatoes; slices of sausage and onion and the inevitable olive oil are then added. Worcester sauce, called *sauce inglês* sometimes adds an ex-patriate refinement.

Thanks to Henry the Navigator, the inhabitants of Oporto have always been known as "Tripeiros", the tripe-eaters, because, when he organized sea voyages from Oporto and the ships were being loaded, he ordered all the meat available to be put on board for the crew and left only the tripes behind. Naturally, many ways were found for using them up. Nowadays, tripe is usually served here with haricot beans and smoked sausage but there are numerous recipes. *Tripes à moda do Porto* is possibly the best known.

There are several excellent restaurants specialising in fish in Matosinhos and Leça, just north of Oporto, and in the city some traditional and new restaurants are ideal to explore good Portuguese cooking.

Apart from the sturdy bacalhau, the expensive lobsters and the larger than life sardines (which are too big to be tinned), the most usual fish to be served are *pescada frite* (fried hake) and *linguado* (sole).

Meat dishes vary, from the basic *cozido* (meat stew) and popular *frango* (chicken dishes) to *bifes* (steaks), *cabrito* (kid) and *febras de porco* (leg of pork), cooked in wine and spices. Rice (*arroz*) or potatoes (*batatas*) are always served with meat and usually a green or tomato salad accompanies them. Beware when eating in someone's home because it is usual for each course to be offered twice; take a little rather than the customary English helping to begin with.

Try to leave room for the dessert course. Strangely, it is here that the Portuguese have used most of their imagination in creating sensational, different dishes. Eggs, almonds and sugar are the main ingredients for these desserts that enjoy such romantic names as *foguetes* (rockets) and *papos de anjo* (angel's breasts). Apple tarts (*torta*) are also appetising, though not so regional as the varieties of *pudim* that are always available.

Portugal is not a great cheese-producing or cheese-eating nation. The associations of port and cheese are stronger in the consuming country of the U.K. than in the producing country of Portugal. The two cheeses most in evidence in the north are *queija de serra* (mountain cheese) which is runny during the winter months and hard in the summer, and comes from the Serra da Estrela, and the *queija das ilhas* (cheese of the islands) which comes from the Azores and is stronger and harder. *Queijo do Alentejo* is another slightly hard ewe milk cheese. Portuguese Brie and Camembert are also becoming known and appreciated. Cheese, when it is served, comes last.

A delicious accompaniment to the cheese is *marmelada* (quince preserve). A slice of this orange coloured jelly-like sweet, shaped like a Christmas pudding, enhances the cheese enormously – a native dish that is totally at home in its own surroundings (it is no relation at all to marmalade).

Wine in restaurants

Most restaurants offer an amazing choice of wines. They may not have in stock all that they list but whatever they do have you can be sure that it will be tremendous value for money. They always make a distinction between *vinhos verdes* (young wines) and *vinhos maduros* (matured wines). Vinhos verdes are both red and white, although only the latter are generally exported. Red vinhos verdes are tough, harsh wines, reminiscent of the sort of country wine you might drink straight from the cask; they often throw a sediment and I have often seen neat serried rows of emptied glasses well sedimented in the excellent restaurant Zé do Calçada (Joseph of the Staircase), in Amarante.

The matured wines can also be red or white. The best come from the Dão area, but it is always well worthwhile experimenting with different ones that may be recommended. Often a purely local wine can be surprisingly good and cheap. Port, on the other hand, is always expensive in restaurants. It is seldom used in cooking, but always available to drink, either a dry white as an aperitif or an old tawny after the meal.

As with all enjoyment of food and wine in places away from home, it is tempting to try to reproduce recipes and wines when you are back home. But because of the native, introvert style of Portuguese cooking, Portuguese dishes and their wines are sometimes perhaps more difficult to enjoy outside their normal environment than dishes from other countries. Try by all means, but remember that it is we who change in our predilections from country to country not so much the food or the wine. There are various collections of Portuguese recipes, but few are in English.

The region's table wines

Apart from port, Portugal's best known wine export is the pétillant pink wine, Mateus Rosé, which has been a gigantic success both for the Guedes family, who own it, and for the novice wine consumer. The quality of the wine and continual promotion of the brand have ensured that Mateus still outstrips its competitors and blazes the way for potential wine lovers to have a pleasant introduction to drinking.

The blandness of the drink however does not lend itself (nor is it intended to) to accompanying local specialities which may in part explain why Portuguese cuisine is so little known outside Portugal, even though Mateus Rosé is world famous. However, Portugal does also produce two quite different, highly pleasing *appellation contrôlée* wines that are beginning to make an impact in export markets: Dão and Vinho Verde.

Dão wines are produced around Viseu, south of the Douro Valley. They respect strict *appellation contrôlée* rules governing cultivation and vinification, and during a stay in north Portugal there are so many differently produced Dãos that these round, earthy yet velvety wines can be thoroughly explored. Much of the wine is made in co-operatives and the old-fashioned town of Viseu is an ideal base for visiting the vineyards and co-operatives, especially the Sogrape Winery in the town itself.

All Dão wines are classified as *vinhos maduros*, but that is no reason why you cannot drink the white Dão wine while it is young, choosing the oldest Dão red available to take full advantage of its maturity. Dão wines are usually bottled after spending four years in cask.

Vinho Verde is produced in the Minho district, and is always slightly *pétillant*, with a low alcoholic strength of between 8° to 11.5° alcohol by volume. The vines are strung up on trees or high trellises so as to enable a second crop to be grown underneath in the same area. The malic acid content in these wines is so high that it cannot be all eliminated, as it is with other wines, during the secondary fermentation process. The result is that a forced malo-lactic secondary fermentation is employed to reduce it and convert it into the smoother tasting lactic. Carbon dioxide is formed, later freed and then retained in the bottle, giving the wine, both red and white, a slight sparkle. But there are considerable variations in the amount of *pétillance* from maker to maker.

Portuguese fully sparkling wines are pleasant, if slightly sweet. When chilled, they may be enjoyed on a hot summer's day. They may be made by either the Champagne or sealed vat processes.

The other four wine regions in Portugal are all in the south – Bucelas, Carcavelos, Colares and Setúbal.

Spirits

There are two principal spirits produced and consumed in Portugal, brandy and *bagaçeira*. Neither is exported in any great quantity, so they are ideal drinks to try during a visit. Brandy is produced in distilleries by all the larger wineries, and is available at every café, bar, restaurant, hotel and retail spirit store. Portuguese brandy is made by a single distillation of the wine in a simple copper pot still. Brands vary, from those that taste too much of vanilla to a version resembling a respectable alternative to Armagnac. Price and experimental tastings will lead you to the one you like. Most port shippers have their own brandy, as they do their own *bagaçeira*.

Bagaçeira corresponds to the French *marc*. Its name would be more meaningful if it was called "Bagaçeira do Porto" as in "Marc de Champagne", but it is not. It is a white spirit, ferocious in its bite, which is made by distilling all the leftovers from making port, such as the pips and the stalks of the grape, that have done their work but are not allowed to rest. The quantity of bagaçeira produced each year is thus directly proportional to the amount of wine that has been made. Smell before you drink . . . A very harsh, immature spirit will announce its flavour by the way it presents itself to the nose.

Whisky, gin and vodka are all produced locally in Portugal and are generally very good value as compared to the imported brands, which carry a high duty and are therefore expensive.

XI
Other Ports from Other Countries

PORT COMES ONLY from Portugal. That is what Portuguese authorities in Oporto would like to have us believe and recognize. But wines labelled "port" are also produced and drunk in other wine-growing areas of the world, notably Australia, North America and South Africa. Of course, it is not proper port made in the Douro Valley, but it is port to those Australians, Americans and South Africans who buy and enjoy their native red dessert wines.

The vine moved to the New World with the early missionaries. Vine cuttings were taken to Mexico around 1520; thence to Argentina and Peru. The first vines in South Africa were planted by the Dutch in 1655; missionaries had planted in California by 1697. The Antipodes were the last to get vines; Australia had to wait until 1788. But by 1850, wine growing had become firmly established in these countries. Over the years, it was natural for wine producers outside the traditional European vine-growing regions to call their table wines or fortified wines by the names, already well known, of the wines that they tried to emulate, whether or not they used the same grapes. Burgundy, Chablis, Sauternes, sherry and, of course, port, all became firmly part of each country's wine industry. Although flattering to the original European geographical areas, international marketing today calls for more rigorous labelling. Today, some twenty million cases of wines labelled port are consumed each year, throughout the world. Of these, only seven million are produced in the Douro Valley in Portugal.

André Brink, in his book *Dessert Wine in South Africa*, claims that "today it is widely accepted that the name [port] has lost its exclusive geographic connotation, referring rather to a particular style of wine, the produce of a particular process." Those of us involved in the port trade in Europe would deny this, but there is no disputing the sheer size of other countries' port production.

Port is a protected wine only in Europe and, since 1968, in the United States. There, port produced and bottled in Portugal is called porto, as it is in Portugal itself and in the French-speaking countries. The main concern for the misuse of the word port is that in the United States the vast majority of port produced is cheap red dessert wine, which does no good for the image and reputation of true port from Portugal. In the United States, fortified wines, whether dry or sweet, are called dessert wines. Twenty years ago, dessert wines, which were often drunk for alcohol rather than pleasure, represented three-quarters of all wine sales in the United States. Sales have declined tremendously and these wines now represent less than one quarter of sales. Recently however, quality port has been produced in small quantities in California and this industry could well expand. Australia and South Africa have always produced good, well-balanced ports and New Zealand has begun to do so.

United States

Eight million cases of American-made port were consumed in the United States in 1980, but sales are declining steadily as the trend is towards table wines. The main differences between "domestic port" and "imported port" (porto) are the grape varieties used, the sun and rain ratios, the soil and the fermentation processes. Californian port has traditionally been made with the heavy sweet Tinta Madera grape variety. Ninety-eight per cent has been grown in the burning heat of the San Joaquin Valley, due east and inland from San Francisco. The grapes were allowed to become over-ripe because the growers were paid on the sugar content. The result was a grapey raisin taste. Newcomers to the Californian port scene are now using table wine grape varietals. Even so, some varietals get to over 15 per cent naturally, without fortification. When I asked the Wine Institute in San Francisco how this was, the reply came back: "They just leave 'em out there and pray".

E. & J. Gallo are the largest producers of port in the United States, although The Christian Brothers produce the largest premium volume in this sector. Being a family owned concern, Gallo are not required to release any sales statistics. Still run by the two founders, brothers Ernest, responsible for marketing, and Julius, responsible for production, Gallo is the most powerful wine company in the States today. They use Carignane, the indigenous Zinfandel, Tinta Madera and some Grenache grapes. They have also developed two *vinifera* hybrids, Rubired and Royalty, at the University of California at Davis, specifically for port production. During any one year, Gallo probably produce as much port in Modesto, California, as all the port shippers put together do in the Douro Valley. The size of operations is immense. They transport the freshly picked grapes in twenty-ton gondola tank lorries. The grapes are then crushed, and centrifugally pumped into 100,000-gallon fermentation tanks where frequent pumping is carried out to extract the proper amount of colour from the skins. Neutral grape spirit is added at the desired critical time to arrest fermentation and the resultant port is 18°–19° alcohol by volume.

Mass-produced certainly, although there is nothing intrinsically wrong in that, but the wines, although well-made, lack the personality and finesse of port; certain elements can be changed, others cannot. The classic wine-grape varieties, such as Cabernet Sauvignon, Zinfandel and Petite Sirah, are now being used with great success and perhaps California's soil and micro-climate favour these grapes over the traditional varieties of the Douro. Most port is produced, not in the cool coastal regions, but south and inland of San Francisco in the Central Valley where the sun is torrid and constant. The soil is fertile and the land flat, so the vine has an easy life; it ¹oes not have to struggle for survival as it does in the Douro Valley. The result is that the ports produced in California traditionally have a rather cooked nose and a grapey taste.

Today, there are more than fifty wineries in the United States, well over half in California, producing port-style wines. Other port producing states include Arkansas, Georgia, Illinois, Michigan, Missouri, New Jersey, New York, Ohio and Washington. Many produce less than 5,000 cases of port; a few, over 250,000 cases p.a. The largest producers are E. & J. Gallo, Paul Masson, Christian Brothers, United Vintners (all in California) and Taylor (in New York). Most producers other than those in California and New York sell primarily in their own home state.

The encouraging aspects about the California wine industry are that it has little tradition to inhibit positive growth and, as a result, many new wine-makers are constantly on the lookout to experiment. I first visited California in 1973 when many wine-makers had got to the stage when they knew they could produce first-class wines, thanks in part to exhaustive studies at the University of California at Davis. The wines then were, in general, correctly made but bland and lacking in character. The watershed has now been firmly crossed, and on subsequent visits I have been delightfully impressed by the advances made and the startling rapidity of new wine-producers coming on the scene.

Although most large American wineries still produce ports labelled simply "ruby" and "tawny", several established wineries in California, such as The Christian Brothers and Beringer, the latter now owned by Nestlé, have begun to experiment with vintage dated ports. The Christian Brothers brought out a 1969 and 1973, but aged in wood, not in bottle. Beringer produced a Cabernet Sauvignon vintage-dated port in 1979.

Meanwhile, since the late 1940s, Ficklin, in Madera, just north of Fresno, had been traditionally recognized as producing the Californian port closest to Portuguese port. This is partly achieved by using certain Portuguese grape varietals and their blend is always constant, uninterrupted by vintage-dated embellishments. Every time I have tasted Ficklin, I recognize its quality, but it is still a different animal from its Douro Valley namesake. I find it to be slightly raisiny, but the style is always steady and the result is a well-balanced generous dessert wine.

As with most quality port wines produced in California, consumption is mainly in California itself and is elsewhere restricted to a few major cities, especially New York.

The Boutique winery explosion in the 1970s also threw up three specialist companies determined to produce classic vintage-dated ports. These entrepreneurial fashion-conscious wine-makers regarded quality as being so much more important than quantity. From a small base, each has emulated, in its individual way, the salient characteristics of vintage port.

Jim Olson of J. W. Morris Port Works decided to produce port in California after the Revolution in Portugal in 1974, thinking that problems in Portugal might encourage production of traditional vintage port in California. The concept that the foothills of Sierra Nevada were geographically similar to parts of the Douro Valley spurred him on. The grapes he uses are the Zinfandel and Ruby Cabernet; he believes in using classic wine varieties rather than table and raisin grapes, traditionally favoured by Central Valley wineries.

The first blend produced was called Founders Port, maybe respecting Portuguese antecedents, and J. W. Morris are now producing vintage, the first being 1977 and late-bottled vintage ports, the latter spending four years in American oak casks. J. W. Morris represent, with Quady and Woodbury, the first tiny, but serious, glimmer of "Portuguese port" light ever in this enormous country. Founders Port is totally different from all mass-produced California ports as selected grape varietals are used, open-top Redwood fermenting tanks are used and traditional port tastes are lovingly respected. The wines are fruity and young, sensual and fragrant. Gone is the dreaded grapey raisin hallmark of cheap California ports.

Based in Madera, Andrew Quady produced his first vintage port in 1975. He made 1,600 cases then; by 1979 he had doubled his production and was able to sell outside California. Such is the embryonic state of proper California port, that each year sees a different experiment in production. Quady selected Amador County for his vineyards as he believes that Amador Zinfandels have the necessary grip and spice that is needed for a port. He maintains that "grapes, fortifying brandy and barrel make port".

Woodbury Winery is a new family winery in Marin County specializing in the production of fine California port. Russell Woodbury firmly believes that with selected old vine grape varietals, such as the Petite Sirah, Zinfandel, Pinot Noir and Cabernet Sauvignon, using the cooler coastal California climate north of San Francisco, making his own finest still brandy for fortification and using the production techniques employed in Portugal, he can produce the rich long-lived ports in the tradition of the great vintage ports of the Alto Douro in quality seven years in ten, as opposed to Portugal's average of three in ten. Woodbury will make a traditional vintage port – bottled two years after the vintage – in these fine years; He uses California as the appellation, picks only in the mornings at vintage time, crushes in the field and fortifies to 20 per cent alcohol by volume. I tasted the 1977 vintage in San Francisco in 1979 and found the colour very full and robust. There was a definite vintage port grip, a keen stalkiness that gave the wine a backbone that has never been achieved in California before. Woodbury produced 600 cases of his first 1977 vintage and has now increased to 5,000 cases for the 1980.

This new generation of port men and their followers could really do for Californian port what their predecessors have already, but only recently, done for California table wines. California, with its fertile valleys, coastal breezes, blue skies and informal pace of life, is about as far a cry as you can get from the majestic yet isolated Douro Valley, its abrupt climate, its traditional way of life and classic styles. But now that the "grapey raisin" characteristics have been identified, the sky could be California's limit.

South Africa

"Port? . . . Easiest thing in the world. All you have got to do is pick and press, you stir the must and remove the husks, you pour the must on the spirits waiting in the tank – and then you can sit back and relax."

According to André Brink in his *Dessert Wine in South Africa*, that is the stock answer the wine farmers in South Africa give when asked about making port or any sweet wine. A refinement came from one farmer: "Show me a vineyard from where you can see the sea and I will show you where you can make good port".

In spite of this relaxed confidence that South Africans seem to have when discussing port, they produce and consume around one million cases per annum in varying degrees of quality and styles.

The geographical area most suited for port production is the Cape coastal belt, between the undulating mountain ranges and Cape Town. The rainfall is exactly the same as around Pinhão in the Douro Valley, 50 cm to 80 cm per annum. The rolling hills allow the water to run off, so keeping the soil lean and hungry and the soil itself embraces Table Mountain sandstone, granite and slate. Most of the ingredients needed for port production are there. The soil is not too fertile so the wines have fullness and grip. The damp sea breezes ensure the necessary humidity needed to stop the wines evaporating too much.

Most leading Portuguese grape varieties were imported into South Africa over fifty years ago. Since then, much experimentation has taken place to see which are most suited to the South African soil and climate. These have emerged as being the Tinta Barroca, accounting for 75 per cent of all vines grown in Stellenbosch, Malmesbury and Paarl, the Souzão, which gives a full, deep colour, and the Pontac, which was the basis of the famous Old Constantia Red.

The leading producers of South African port are the huge wine-growers' cooperative, KWV, founded in 1918 – selling under their famous Paarl label – and the Cape Wine & Distillers Company. The main quality brands that you see in the shops are Sedgwicks, Oude Heerengracht, Drostdy, Morris and Bertrams. The market is divided into two categories – high priced and low priced ports. The leading low priced brand is Apex Cape. Possibly the most famous estate making port is Allesverloren, the property of the Malan family.

The most popular styles of port are ruby, tawny, vintage and then white port. The basic difference between ruby and tawny is that ruby is matured for five years in huge wooden vats, each containing 10,000 litres, whereas tawny is matured for seven years in wooden pipes of 500 litres. The ruby, therefore, keeps its rich colour, whereas the tawny is in greater contact with wood and so loses more colour. More oxidization takes place and the resulting tawny is both lighter and drier. White port is made from the Stein grape variety and not matured so long.

However, it is of their vintage port that South Africans are justly proud. The great years to look out for are 1943, 1944, 1949, 1952, 1960 and 1961. Like the ruby ports, which after all is what vintage port really is, the choicest wine of selected vintage years is first matured in huge wooden vats. Colour can be preserved this way and, after two years, it is bottled and de facto becomes vintage port. The dark richness of vintage port needs fifteen to twenty years to mature. André Brink aptly describes the final stages of the horizontal vintage port bottle. "It is because of this long, slow maturation that Port needs a day, or at least several hours, to breathe and rid itself of crust and dregs (the tangible symptoms of its claustrophobia) before it can be decanted and poured."

The KWV at Paarl and the Drostdy Cellars at Tulbagh welcome visitors, especially those from South African port's main export markets, the U.K., Canada and Germany.

Australia

Australia has produced sweet red wine, known as port, ever since she started producing wine in the 1820s. The very young fortified wines sold in wine saloons and hotels were known as "fourpenny dark".

The flavour of Australian ports have never been similar to Portuguese ports because they have traditionally been made from existing grape varieties available in large amounts in Australia, i.e. the Shiraz (Syrah), Grenache, Mataro and a small proportion of Muscat. The Shiraz produces the rich colour needed for long maturing wines. The Grenache produces lighter-coloured, scented and quick-maturing wines, whereas the Mataro is something in between. Ports produced from these three main grape varieties were often matured separately and later blended to taste.

The fear of Phylloxera prohibited the introduction of new varieties into Australia for many years, although the two Portuguese varieties, Torriga and Bastardo, have always existed in the Rutherglen/ Corowa inland pocket on the Murray River. This area straddling the two states of New South Wales and Victoria has always produced finest quality Australian port.

Annual sales of all qualities are about two million cases, representing 6 per cent of total wine consumption.

Unlike South Africa, but like Portugal, the main port producing areas are out of sight of the sea, and alongside one of the country's leading rivers. Like the River Douro, the Murray River flows east to west. It rises in the Australian Alps just south of Canberra and charts its way, acting as the state border between New South Wales and Victoria, through to Adelaide in South Australia.

The main port producing regions along the Murray River are:

> Renmark, Bevvi, Loxton, Waikerie in South Australia; Mildura, Robinvale, Swan Hill, Sheparton, Corowa, and Rutherglen in New South Wales and Victoria.

The third principal area is the Riverina district along the Murrumbidgee River centred around Griffith and Leeton in New South Wales. These regions traditionally have produced good strong dessert wines. With the trend towards light wines, this dessert wine market has halved in the last twenty years. Vineyards became geared to producing table wines and premium port production has evolved in the well-known Barossa Valley in South Australia, and Glenrowan and Milawa in north-eastern Victoria.

The classic table wine area around the Hunter Valley used to produce port until the 1950s. Since then, table wine has become so popular that little port is produced there now. Also, the climatic conditions there are less favourably disposed towards port.

Ruby port, because of its historical cheap connotation is rarely found and is not a popular style in Australia. The market divides into two, tawny and vintage.

There is an Australian style of tawny port which has become the norm. It should not be confused with its Portuguese counterpart, as Australian port has developed sufficiently and, at times pleasingly, to stand on its own feet. The most popular tawny ports are big in fruit, slightly raisiny, often luscious with a low acid finish. Seppelts Para Liqueur ports (vintage dated) are supreme examples of this style. In the 1970s there was a manic rush to collect these old tawny ports and a bottle of hundred-year-old Para tawny fetched Aust. $4,000 at auction. Seppelt's Para is made from Shiraz, Mataro and Grenache grapes and owes its name to the North Para river, which meanders through the Barossa Valley near Adelaide. These old tawnies taste rather like a luscious nutty liqueur with a concentrated, almost burnt, fruity aroma.

Australian ports at their best exhibit characteristics which put them in world class as beverages in their own right; the hope is that more and more producers will follow the quality path.

The best known quality tawny brands are Seppelt Para 102, Yalumba Galway Pipe, Penfold's Grandfather, Hardy's Bin M45 and Lindeman's RF1.

Vintage port, or the so-called vintage style of port, has long been produced in Australia. The grape varieties used are mainly the Shiraz and Cabernet Sauvignon. Unfortunately legislation is not conducive to the production of fine vintage ports. The minimum strength is 17 per cent alcohol by volume and vintage ports are often bottled after only twelve months. Consequently there is a plethora of young ruby wines on the market with a "vintage" year on the label. Unlike true vintage ports, they do not command high prices and similar-priced tawny ports are much better value.

The cheaper vintage ports often have a jammy sweet fruit character with a soft finish. This is the typical Australian traditional taste. Latterly, as demand for quality has increased, certain companies, such as Hardy, Yalumba, Lindeman's and Stanley Leasingham have been producing vintage ports much more along the lines of true Portuguese vintage ports. They are all drunk sooner than their Portuguese counterpart, but are aiming at getting the beautiful purple red colour, and stalky character with an astringent finish.

Comparative port tasting

In March 1980, I organised a comparative tasting in London of ports from other countries. The objective was to evaluate "blind" quality non-Portuguese ports from the three main regions: Australia, California, and South Africa. Ten of us, comprising a Master of Wine, established port tasters, and experienced wine writers, tasted twelve such ports.

This was probably the first such tasting ever to be held, as although Australia and South Africa have been producing good quality ports for many years, innovative wine entrepreneurs only began to produce vintage ports in California in the mid-1970s. Thus, the Californian ports we tasted were "hot off the press".

Australia was represented by Hardy's Fine Old Tawny, Para 102 Tawny, Penfolds Old Tawny, and Yalumba Director's Special; California, by Ficklin, Quady 1977 vintage, J. W. Morris 1976 vintage, and Woodbury 1977 vintage; and South Africa, by Old Cape Colony, SAWF Medium Tawny and a 1944 vintage. The ports varied from young to old, tawny to vintage and £1·49 per bottle to £12·80 per bottle retail in the U.K. Most people agreed that whilst they were not proper ports, they could be grouped by family resemblances.

The Australian ports had most maturity, were full, round, slightly sweet. They were judged to be the best non-ports. The amazing Para stood out, dramatic in its hot wooded liqueurishness. The Californian ports had an obvious fruitiness, and a hot earth nose about them. They were young and fresh; and there was much conjecture as to when or if their flavoursome characteristics would mature. The South African ports all had a distinctive raisiny taste. Heat and warmth combined with flowery, delicate, soft sensations.

XII
World Markets

HISTORICALLY, THE NATURAL style of port has been ruby. The deep, rich red ports of the eighteenth and nineteenth centuries, trodden by feet and cut with aguardente (brandy), were enjoyed in their main market, England, as ruby. It was cold in those days. There was no central heating. Men and women physically worked harder than they do today. They needed a warming drink, especially during the long winter months.

Young ruby port fitted the bill admirably. Consumed in quantity at home and in the taverns, by rich and poor folk equally, port was the drink made by Englishmen for Englishmen. Vintage port was an extension of young, ruby port; conceived as a quality ruby port to be enjoyed in style by the gentry of Old England.

The basic differences between the British companies and the Portuguese companies during this time were style and quality. The British companies had a ready-made consumer market – England. The Portuguese did not really understand the port trade. Their own home market did not have the climatic conditions nor the lifestyle to appreciate the unique characteristics of port. The English in Oporto had to react to quality control in one form or another from their customers in England. They had to be competitive. The Portuguese shippers, on the other hand, did not have the pressure to keep to an accepted standard of quality. Continuous demand enabled the British shippers to produce crisp, clean, ruby ports, whereas the Portuguese shippers tended to leave their ports longer in wood, not rack them so often and thus, in the main, produced lazier tawny ports.

Nowadays British and Portuguese companies alike have sufficient technical expertise and consumer awareness to produce any style of port that they need. The British style and the Portuguese styles of port have largely disappeared, except in vintage port. Entrenched, long-established buying positions and traditional know-how firmly establishes the British shippers, with the exception of the two fine Portuguese companies, Noval and Ferreira, as leaders in producing vintage port.

Towards the end of the nineteenth century, other northern countries were taking an interest in port. The Scandinavians, obviously feeling the cold more than anyone else, became big buyers of port.

Ernest Cockburn, writing up his "historical notes since 1860", records that whilst Mr Gladstone was being lobbied in the House of Commons by a wine committee not to increase wine duties, other markets were also reassessing the impact of port in their countries.

There is a cryptic entry for 1881:

> The demand for Port Wine in North Germany at this period is not interesting as the styles required seemed to call for a large range of flavours extraneous to port which the trade sought to satisfy by various means.

Under 1882:

> Business in the USA in Port wine was at this time not easy in view of the apathy of the wine merchants to the wine, which was usually consumed by the better class of people solely on medical advice, whilst the poorer classes substituted Tarragona or Californian wines.

I cannot resist the next entry, which showed the business-like approach in those slow moving days: "In these days the letter post left London for Oporto at 1 p.m., which was doubtless inconvenient, but it took only 5 days, which was considered fast." I suppose the only real difference is that now a letter still takes five days, but that it is considered slow.

In 1883:

> In May, Sweden lowered the maximum strength at which importations of Port wine could be made to that country from 21 degrees to 20 degrees.

The most telling entry comes under 1884:

> In July there was a cholera scare in France, which to some seemed an opening for Port wine, as, when Russia experienced a similar epidemic, a large trade in Port wine had been built up there on the ground that good red Port wine was both a restorative and preventative. It was, however, not anticipated that equal success would be met with in France, as in that country the importation strength was low, whereas the wine required for the purpose should be possessed of both body and tannin, each of which needed alcoholic support.

France is, of course, now the No. 1 port market. The country which produces the finest table wine in the world is also the leading export market for port. The cholera scare of 1884 may have sparked off an interest in the unique properties in port in the minds of the health conscious French, but other factors are more credible.

More port was consumed in the world in 1925 than in any other year before or since. The Second World War savaged the U.K. port market. In the meantime, the Portuguese shippers were finding that France was becoming a natural outlet for their lighter ports. Port was cheap enough and different enough to become fashionable. In the 1950s, the British shippers were also looking at France and Continental Europe in general to become customers for their ports now that the British market had necessarily been cut back.

In 1963, that great vintage in Portugal, France, for the first time, imported more port than the U.K. Since then, the port market in France has grown and grown. France now consumes more than 2 million cases to the U.K.'s less than 1 million cases each year. These two countries account for over 50 per cent of all port exports. The strange thing is that the French drink port as the British drink sherry – as an aperitif. In consequence, sherry sales in France are negligible. The French find it equally strange that the British drink and seemingly enjoy port after meals. They believe, with their refined gourmet taste, that the best drink to have after meals is a spirit digestif. Port, on the other hand, makes an ideal soft, round aperitif leading into the inevitable bottle(s) of wine. The ports they drink are almost exclusively tawny (80 per cent) and white port (20 per cent). Ruby and vintage ports are largely unknown.

Every product category needs a standard bearer. The image of a particular product lives or dies by the top quality within the category. If there is no top quality, then the image suffers. The image suffers and no-one takes pleasure in giving or drinking that product. The product dies. So it is with port.

The flagship for port in the U.K., traditionally, has been vintage port. The great vintage port names conjure up a Who's Who in Port; they are above commercial styles. Now in the U.K., there is a trend towards old tawny ports as representing today's fashion towards lightness. In France, and in her neighbouring aperitif market, Belgium, the Portuguese shippers similarly need, as does the consumer, a premium quality port to uphold the image of the category. Dated tawny ports (1937 bottled 1978) and ports with age indication (aged for twenty years in wood) are examples of achieving this.

Port's top ten markets account for 95 per cent of all sales. Apart from Russia, who started reimporting port in 1976 after the Portuguese Revolution in 1974, all these countries are in Europe. They are, in order, France, Portugal, U.K., Belgium, Netherlands, Germany, Italy, Denmark, U.S.S.R. and Switzerland. Owing to high taxes and monopoly trading, sales in Norway and Sweden have gradually declined in importance and Switzerland, at one time a big importer of white port, found the cost too high for a regular aperitif, and additive to their own light wine.

Continental Europe can be divided into two, regarding consumption of different styles of port. Northern Europe basically still drinks ruby, whereas Southern Europe prefers the lighter tawny styles. Having said that, as with the original differences between British styles of port and Portuguese styles of port, modern trading methods have tended to create international brands that transcend these historical patterns.

The individual style of each company, whether it be British in origin or Portuguese, is now more expressed by the exterior image of the product rather than by the port style itself. Each company has its premium port, Cockburn's Special Reserve, Croft Distinction, Fonseca Bin 27, Noval LB, Sandeman's Partners, Taylor's Late Bottled Vintage Reserve or Warre's Warrior, which it advertises and promotes. Each company also has its standard ruby and tawny blends which sell more in quantity, but which need the premium brands to sell their quality image to the consumer.

These are all called wood ports, as opposed to vintage ports. I am not endeared to the term "wood ports" and I studiously try to avoid using it. It means that they are aged in wood, rather than in bottle, which I find attractive, but the term wood ports, used universally throughout the trade, does not appeal to me. Imagine "wood sherries". Not a pleasing term. I prefer the two styles as "port" and "vintage port". Having established that distinction, whilst the latter always have driven corks that need to be extracted with a corkscrew, the former have stopper corks. Once opened a bottle of port will remain perfectly healthy and full-flavoured for some considerable time, provided that it is firmly re-stoppered. The bigger the air-space in the bottle, the faster the oxidization. So a partly-filled bottle of port, if left for months rather than weeks, will, in due course, gradually lose its freshness and become slightly tired.

The costs of producing port in the Douro Valley will always remain high. For this reason, premium quality brands sold on an international basis will become the policy pursued by most farsighted port shippers for the remainder of the twentieth century. After that, who knows?

In 1981 eighty-five countries imported port direct from Portugal, an increasing amount, now over 60 per cent, being bottled in the shippers' lodges in Portugal. The main areas and those with potential can be subdivided.

Europe

The E.E.C. countries take 90 per cent. France, Germany and Belgium drink mostly tawny and white port. The U.K. drinks mostly ruby. Italy prohibits the import of port in bulk, so all her imports are in bottle. The Italians often enjoy their port fashionably in fruits and fruit salads. Since she abandoned quota restriction in 1972, Italy is now the seventh port market. Consumption in Austria and Switzerland is small; the latter still imposes taxes on all imports by weight, so most port is shipped in bulk and bottled there. The Netherlands, whilst leading the world in drinking dry sherry, prefer their port to be ruby. The trade in Norway, Sweden and Finland is controlled by Government monopolies and so the choice is restricted to old-fashioned listings. Taxes are very high, so sales have declined. Denmark, with its traditional wine trade, likes ruby port and has the highest per capita consumption of port in the world. The Irish enjoy vintage port, but most of the sales are in the tawny style. Portugal itself consumes dry white port as an aperitif and all shades of red port at all other times of the day.

Port is being consumed more and more at home and being bought more and more in hyper- and super-markets and chain stores, rather than the traditional specialist.

North America

The U.S.A. imports very little port, although there is always considered enormous potential just around the corner. When, rather than *if*, the U.S.A. does take to port, it could be an exciting explosion. Port is mostly consumed in New York City, California and Chicago.

Canada, through its independent State Liquor Control Boards, imports about 25 per cent of what its southern neighbour imports. As in Norway and Sweden, the liquor stores are so anonymous and unconducive to buying anything, that sales are declining. No promotion within the stores is allowed, so no image can be portrayed.

South America

All countries buy port from time to time, more depending on their own economies than on consumer demand. Brazil buys port mainly from Portuguese shippers, reflecting her Portuguese ancestry. Venezuela happily imports tawny port on a regular basis.

Africa

The success of port sales in France has encouraged the former French West African countries, such as the Camerouns, Senegal and others, regularly to import those brands that are popular in France. South Africa imports a little port, depending on licence availability.

Before the 1974 Revolution, the Portuguese colonies, notably Angola and Mozambique, imported considerable quantities of port and brandy. This trade has now declined.

Far East

Hong Kong and Macau are the biggest customers of port in this huge geographical area. The Chinese belief that red wine gives virility and health, especially to mothers who have just given birth, helps port sales. To bring a new mother a bottle of port, preferably the most expensive you can find, is a great tribute and honoured gesture. The tiny island of Macau, being a Portuguese colony, with its galaxy of retail shops all juxtapositioned, drinks about three times as much as Hong Kong.

Australasia

Australia and New Zealand have similar drinking habits to the U.K. A port after a meal is normal rather than not. As their own domestic ports can be so good, only the older tawny and vintage ports make headway in this market. The cigar-shaped island of New Caledonia, being a French possession, is also fond of port as an aperitif and imports a regular quantity each year.

So the world's annual consumption of some 80 million bottles of port is varied and spread throughout the globe. The conversational wine that starts in the majestic Douro mountains finds its way into glasses held by a complete cross-section of the western world.

Typical Port Labels

Classic vintage port label showing the bottling date two years after the vintage

Late bottled vintage ports, bottled between four and six years after the vintages are becoming increasingly popular

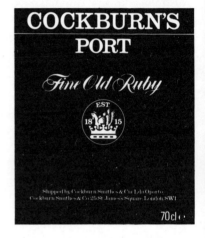

Ruby or tawny ports indicate colour and intensity variances. These are standard wood ports and form the backbone of each shippers reserves

Portugal

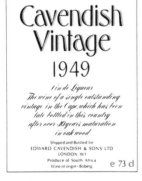

South Africa

California

Australia

Appendix i:
Further Reading

CHARLES SELLERS' *Oporto, Old and New*, published in 1899, is marvellously dated, yet immensely relevant to the thinking of the port trade up to the end of the nineteenth century. It is a collector's item, but should be found in the better wine libraries. It is indicative of the long life-cycle of port that many of his descriptions of the port companies and their quintas remain valid today.

The 1970s saw a resurgence of books on port, starting with Sarah Bradford's *The Story of Port – the Englishman's Wine*. Christie's Wine Publications published a new and revised edition in 1978. It covers the history of port and the port trade today with admirable clarity.

George Robertson's *Port* in the Faber series edited by Julian Jeffs, was also published in 1978. *Port* is the definitive technical work and an essential reference book for the serious wine student.

Wyndham Fletcher's *Port – an Introduction to its History and Delights*, published by Sotheby's, and Oliver Knox's *Croft, a Journey of Confidence* (Collins) are two different treatments of two of the great port companies, Cockburn and Croft.

John Delaforce's *The Factory House at Oporto*, from Christie's Wine Publications, gives detailed information regarding the history and contents of that unique institution.

Alexis Bespaloff's *The Fireside Book of Wine*, published by Simon and Schuster in New York, is an excellent anthology for wine drinkers and a useful addition to any wine library.

In the Pitman guide series, Jan Read's *Guide to the Wines of Spain and Portugal* provides much complementary information and together with Anthony Hogg's indispensable *Guide to Visiting Vineyards*, published by Michael Joseph, should be read beforehand and taken on your visit to Portugal. The most useful and complete road map of Portugal I found was of the foldup variety sponsored by the Caixa Geral de Depósitos and issued by the Portuguese National Tourist Office, 1 New Bond Street, London, W1.

Appendix ii: Glossary of Wine Terms

Adega:	the building in which the wine is made.
Aguardente:	neutral grape spirit used for fortifying port.
Almudes:	25.4 litres. Twenty-one almudes equal one pipe.
Armazem:	warehouse for storing wine.
Bagaçeira:	fiery white grape spirit, "marc", distilled from the dried pips and skins of the grapes after the vintage.
Balseiro:	cylindrical wooden vat, tapering off at the top and supported by stout legs. Used for maturing port.
Barco rabelo:	traditional Douro single-sail boats used for transporting the six-month-old port from the Douro Valley to Vila Nova de Gaia. They were adapted with shallow draft to navigate the shallows and rapids of the Upper Douro.
Escritório:	office.
Fining:	the clarification of the wine before shipping: particles of tartrates etc. which cloud the wine are removed, usually by refrigeration.
Garafa:	bottle.
Geropiga:	sweet port used in blending for sweetening the wines.
Lagar:	traditional stone tank used for fermenting the wine by treading. Made of granite, they used to stand on a raised platform above the *adega* floor.
Lees:	sediment deposited by the maturing port on the bottom of the cask or vat.
Lodge:	the port-shipper's lodge is a complex in Vila Nova de Gaia housing offices, storage and tasting rooms.
Lota:	the initial parcel of wine from individual vineyards. Similar lotas are blended together; others are kept apart during their maturation process.

Manta: the cap or carpet-like conglomeration of grape skins
                    and pips which rises to the surface of the juice when
                    fermentation begins.
Must: grape juice before fermentation turns it into wine. The
                    addition of aguardente then turns the wine into port.
Pipe: traditional measure of buying, storing and selling a
                    quantity of port. Pipes are elongated wooden casks.
                    Shipping pipes hold 534 litres; Douro pipes hold 550
                    litres, because the traditional formula is 440 parts of
                    must to 110 parts of brandy; lodge pipes vary between
                    580 and 620 litres.
Quinta: an estate or property which, in the Douro Valley, is
                    synonymous with a vineyard. Some quintas are like
                    French wine châteaux, others are small vineyards
                    with a broken-down house attached.
Racking: drawing the wine off the lees to keep it fresh.
Tonel: Oval wooden vat, with mini-door at the front,
                    holding fifteen to twenty-five pipes in which the wine
                    is kept in the Douro after the vintage.
Vinho do Porto: port.

Appendix iii:
Vintage Ports and their Shippers
from 1870–1980

THE FOLLOWING LIST is divided into two. The first list comprises the top
twelve vintage port shippers and the second list comprises the others.
Although this division is arbitrary, I believe few would disagree funda-
mentally with my chosen dozen. These companies, during the past hundred
years, have consistently produced top-class vintage ports and their standing
at Christie's and Sotheby's justifies their reputation.

The second list comprises valid British port shippers, such as Martinez
and Morgan, but these are the secondary vintage port labels of Cockburn
and Croft respectively. Gould Campbell and Smith Woodhouse are in the
Symington group. Some companies have died out, like Kingston and
Southard. Large and small Portuguese port-shippers are increasingly getting
into the vintage port scene with varying degrees of success.

Not all of them declared each year the others did. Thirty-nine declared the
1970 vintage, whereas only seven declared the 1967. Some years some
produced outstanding wines; other years, others did. These lists do not
include single quinta vintage ports, but it is as complete a list as I can muster.
Some companies in the past have lodged samples with the I.V.P., got
approval, but have not declared a vintage that year. This rare practice,
together with some companies being merged and others using a small
company name just for vintage port, have all been taken into account
wherever possible.

List 1

Cockburn	1870, 1872, 1873, 1875, 1878, 1881, 1884, 1887, 1890, 1894, 1896, 1900, 1904, 1908, 1912, 1927, 1935, 1947, 1950, 1955, 1960, 1963, 1967, 1970, 1975
Croft	1870, 1872, 1875, 1878, 1881, 1884, 1885, 1887, 1890, 1894, 1896, 1897, 1900, 1904, 1908, 1912, 1917, 1920, 1922, 1924, 1927, 1935, 1942, 1945, 1950, 1955, 1960, 1963, 1966, 1970, 1975, 1977
Da Silva A. J. (Quinta do Noval)	1896, 1900, 1904, 1908, 1912, 1917, 1919, 1920, 1923, 1927, 1931, 1934, 1941, 1942, 1945, 1947, 1948, 1950, 1955, 1958, 1960, 1962, 1963, 1966, 1969, 1970, 1972, 1975, 1978, 1980
Delaforce	1870, 1873, 1875, 1878, 1881, 1884, 1887, 1890, 1894, 1896, 1900, 1904, 1908, 1912, 1917, 1919, 1920, 1927, 1935, 1945, 1947, 1950, 1955, 1958, 1960, 1963, 1966, 1970, 1975, 1977
Dow	1870, 1872, 1873, 1875, 1878, 1881, 1884, 1887, 1890, 1892, 1896, 1899, 1904, 1908, 1912, 1917, 1919, 1920, 1924, 1927, 1931, 1934, 1935, 1945, 1947, 1950, 1955, 1960, 1963, 1966, 1970, 1972, 1975, 1977, 1980
Ferreira	1894, 1896, 1897, 1900, 1904, 1908, 1912, 1917, 1920, 1924, 1927, 1935, 1937, 1945, 1955, 1960, 1963, 1966, 1970, 1975, 1977, 1980
Fonseca	1870, 1873, 1878, 1881, 1884, 1887, 1890, 1896, 1900, 1904, 1908, 1912, 1920, 1922, 1924, 1927, 1934, 1945, 1948, 1955, 1960, 1963, 1966, 1970, 1975, 1977, 1980

Graham	1870, 1872, 1873, 1875, 1878, 1880, 1881, 1884, 1885, 1887, 1890, 1892, 1894, 1896, 1897, 1900, 1901, 1904, 1908, 1912, 1917, 1920, 1924, 1927, 1935, 1942, 1945, 1948, 1955, 1960, 1963, 1966, 1970, 1975, 1977, 1980
Rebello Valente	1870, 1875, 1878, 1881, 1884, 1887, 1890, 1892, 1894, 1896, 1897, 1900, 1904, 1908, 1911, 1912, 1917, 1920, 1922, 1924, 1927, 1931, 1935, 1942, 1955, 1960, 1963, 1966, 1975, 1980
Sandeman	1870, 1872, 1873, 1875, 1878, 1880, 1881, 1884, 1887, 1890, 1892, 1894, 1896, 1897, 1900, 1904, 1908, 1911, 1912, 1917, 1920, 1927, 1934, 1935, 1942, 1943, 1945, 1947, 1950, 1955, 1957, 1958, 1960, 1962, 1963, 1966, 1967, 1970, 1975, 1977, 1980
Taylor	1870, 1872, 1873, 1875, 1878, 1881, 1884, 1887, 1890, 1892, 1896, 1900, 1904, 1906, 1908, 1912, 1917, 1920, 1924, 1927, 1935, 1940, 1942, 1945, 1948, 1955, 1960, 1963, 1966, 1970, 1975, 1977, 1980
Warre	1870, 1872, 1875, 1878, 1881, 1884, 1887, 1890, 1894, 1896, 1899, 1900, 1904, 1908, 1912, 1917, 1920, 1922, 1924, 1927, 1931, 1934, 1945, 1947, 1950, 1955, 1958, 1960, 1963, 1966, 1970, 1975, 1977, 1980

List 2

Adams	1935, 1945, 1947, 1948, 1950, 1955, 1960, 1963, 1966
Barros, Almeida	1943, 1975
Borges	1914, 1922, 1924, 1963
Burmester	1873, 1878, 1887, 1890, 1896, 1900, 1904, 1908, 1912, 1920, 1922, 1927, 1931, 1935, 1937, 1940, 1943, 1945, 1948, 1954, 1955, 1958, 1960, 1963
Butler, Nephew	1922, 1924, 1927, 1934, 1942, 1945, 1947, 1948, 1955, 1957, 1958, 1960, 1975
Calem	1935, 1947, 1948, 1955, 1958, 1960, 1963, 1975, 1977, 1980
Da Silva C.	1970, 1977, 1978, 1980
Diez	1970, 1975
Dixon	1884, 1887, 1890
Douro Wine Shippers	1970
Feist	1922, 1970
Feuerheerd	1870, 1872, 1873, 1875, 1878, 1881, 1884, 1887, 1890, 1894, 1896, 1900, 1904, 1908, 1912, 1917, 1920, 1924, 1927, 1942, 1943, 1944, 1945, 1951, 1955, 1957, 1960, 1963, 1966, 1970
Guimarãens	1963, 1966, 1970
Gonzalez Byass	1896, 1900, 1904, 1908, 1912, 1917, 1920, 1945, 1955, 1960, 1963, 1967, 1970, 1975
Gould Campbell	1870, 1872, 1873, 1875, 1878, 1881, 1884, 1885, 1887, 1890, 1892, 1896, 1900, 1904, 1908, 1912, 1917, 1920, 1922, 1924, 1927, 1934, 1942, 1955, 1960, 1963, 1966, 1975, 1977, 1980
Hutcheson	1970
Kingston	1922, 1924, 1927

Kopke	1870, 1872, 1873, 1875, 1878, 1881, 1884, 1887, 1890, 1892, 1894, 1896, 1897, 1900, 1904, 1908, 1912, 1917, 1919, 1920, 1922, 1927, 1935, 1945, 1948, 1950, 1952, 1955, 1958, 1960, 1963, 1966, 1970
Mackenzie	1870, 1873, 1875, 1878, 1881, 1884, 1887, 1890, 1896, 1900, 1904, 1908, 1912, 1919, 1920, 1922, 1927, 1935, 1945, 1947, 1948, 1950, 1952, 1954, 1955, 1957, 1958, 1960, 1963, 1966
Martinez	1870, 1872, 1873, 1874, 1875, 1878, 1880, 1881, 1884, 1885, 1886, 1887, 1890, 1892, 1894, 1896, 1897, 1900, 1904, 1908, 1911, 1912, 1919, 1922, 1927, 1931, 1934, 1945, 1955, 1958, 1960, 1963, 1967, 1970, 1975
Messias	1970, 1975
Morgan	1870, 1872, 1873, 1875, 1878, 1881, 1884, 1887, 1890, 1894, 1896, 1900, 1904, 1908, 1912, 1920, 1922, 1924, 1927, 1942, 1948, 1950, 1955, 1960, 1963, 1966, 1970, 1975, 1977
Niepoort	1927, 1945, 1970
Offley Forrester	1870, 1872, 1873, 1874, 1875, 1878, 1881, 1884, 1885, 1887, 1888, 1890, 1892, 1894, 1896, 1897, 1900, 1902, 1904, 1908, 1910, 1912, 1919, 1920, 1922, 1924, 1925, 1927, 1929, 1935, 1950, 1954, 1960, 1962, 1963, 1966, 1967, 1970, 1972, 1975, 1977, 1980
Osborne	1970
Quarles Harris	1927, 1934, 1945, 1947, 1950, 1955, 1958, 1960, 1963, 1966, 1975, 1977, 1980
Pinto dos Santos	1955, 1957, 1958, 1960, 1963, 1966, 1970, 1974, 1975
Poças	1967, 1970, 1975, 1977
Ramos Pinto	1924, 1927, 1945, 1955, 1970
Real Vinicola	1945, 1947, 1950, 1955, 1960
Robertson	1942, 1945, 1947, 1955
Royal Oporto Wine Co.	1934, 1945, 1958, 1960, 1962, 1963, 1967, 1970, 1975
Smith Woodhouse	1870, 1872, 1873, 1875, 1878, 1880, 1881, 1884, 1887, 1890, 1896, 1897, 1900, 1904, 1908, 1912, 1917, 1920, 1924, 1927, 1935, 1945, 1947, 1950, 1955, 1960, 1963, 1966, 1970, 1975, 1977, 1980
Sociedade Constantino	1912, 1927, 1935, 1941, 1945, 1947, 1950, 1958, 1966

Southard	1927
Stormont Tait	1896, 1900, 1904, 1908, 1912, 1920, 1922, 1927
Tuke, Holdsworth	1870, 1873, 1874, 1875, 1881, 1884, 1887, 1890, 1892, 1894, 1896, 1900, 1904, 1906, 1908, 1912, 1917, 1920, 1922, 1924, 1927, 1934, 1935, 1943, 1945, 1947, 1950, 1955, 1960, 1963, 1966
van Zeller	1878, 1881, 1884, 1887, 1890, 1892, 1896, 1904, 1908, 1912, 1917, 1922, 1924, 1927, 1935
Viera de Souza	1970
Wiese & Krohn	1927, 1934, 1935, 1947, 1950, 1952, 1960, 1967, 1970

Index